*Information Security and Employee Behaviour*

# Information Security and Employee Behaviour

*How to Reduce Risk Through Employee Education, Training and Awareness*

ANGUS McILWRAITH

GOWER

Published by
Gower Publishing Limited
Gower House
Croft Road
Aldershot
Hampshire GU11 3HR
England

Gower Publishing Company
Suite 420
101 Cherry Street
Burlington, VT 05401-4405
USA

**British Library Cataloguing in Publication Data**
McIlwraith, Angus
   Information security and employee behaviour : how to reduce
   risk through employee education, training and awareness
   1. Computer security – Management 2. Risk perception
   3. Employees – Attitudes 4. Employees – Training of
   I. Title
   658.4'78

   ISBN: 0 566 08647 6

**Library of Congress Cataloging-in-Publication Data**
McIlwraith, Angus.
   Information security and employee behaviour : how to reduce risk
   through employee education, training and awareness / by Angus
   McIlwraith.
      p. cm.
   Includes bibliographical references and index.
   ISBN 0-566-08647-6
   1. Business enterprises--Computer networks--Security measures.
   2. Information technology--Security measures. 3. Employees
   --Training of.   I. Title
   HD30.38.M35 2005
   658.3'1244--dc22

                                                                    2005023135

Printed and bound in Great Britain by TJ International Ltd, Padstow, Cornwall.

# Contents

# Introduction

*It is clear that many security breaches are the result of human error or negligence resulting from weak operational practices. As any experienced hacker – ethical or criminal – will attest, it is more effective to focus on people errors and poor security practices than it is to try and crack today's sophisticated technology solutions.*

Deloitte – Global Financial Services Industry
2005 Global Security Survey

Information security 'awareness' has been promoted for years as being fundamental to information security practice. In reality, it is something that is often done poorly – so much so that I have seen very limited progress since I started in information security over 20 years ago. To improve this situation requires us (that's you and me, the information security implementation community) to look at awareness in a different way. This book suggests that we are not solely in the security business – we are in the communications and corporate change businesses as well. Changing things is difficult, hence the well-worn quotation from the master:

*It must be considered that there is nothing more difficult to carry out, nor more doubtful of success, nor dangerous to handle, than to initiate a new order of things. For the reformer has enemies and only lukewarm defenders. He must confront the disbelief of mankind, who do not truly believe in anything new until they actually experience it.*

Niccolo di Bernardo dei Machiavelli (1469–1527)

We are fighting the entrenched perceptions of many people, and will suffer the problems Machiavelli[1] states above. This book focuses on implementing lasting, perhaps permanent change within your organization.

There is also considerable emphasis placed on communication. The manner in which information security has been presented by the media has been poor

---

1   Machiavelli was the author of *The Prince*, a guide for politicians and tyrants written in the 16th century. It remains fresh and valid to this day.

– perhaps understandably so in that journalists are by nature generalists and have to relate complex issues rapidly and succinctly. Some of the blame for this misrepresentation has to lie squarely within the information security profession itself. You can argue about why this is so, but the reality is simple. Our historic inability in this area has created a problem that this book seeks, in some part, to address.

Another element within the book is the concept of corporate culture and issues relating to changing it. The change processes relate as much to this area as any other. Culture is an oft-misused term. I hope that my ideas may help you find a way of understanding and then addressing your corporate cultural issues as they relate to information security.

Finally, I am keen to stress that there is no magic bullet to deal with information security issues. The work we are involved in crosses a large number of disciplines and fields, and we have, in order to be successful, to operate in many of them. You need to appreciate that an information security infrastructure is more than network links, servers and software. It includes buildings, documents and, most importantly, people. Messing up when you address people issues will make your professional life a lot more difficult. Dealing with them in a coherent, structured way will ease much of this pain.

## WHAT IS AWARENESS?

For the purposes of this book, awareness is discussed in two parts. The first part is the practice of making people aware of the issues relating to information security. The second part involves encouraging (cajoling, bullying and threatening) them to act in a way that is appropriate to the value of the information they handle as part of their everyday work activities. It is different from training and education. What is apparent is that awareness, training and education practices are unavoidably interlinked.

Many people confuse awareness with publicity, and think that a yearly roadshow or the production of a mouse mat with a slogan printed on it will meet the bill: they will not. Such activities have a place in the panoply of other activities that need to happen if you are to make people truly aware, but they are by no means the total picture.

It is the second part (encouraging people to change the way they do things) that makes the difference. The core of the ideas in this book centres on behaviour. There are certain behaviours we want to happen, and others that we do not want to happen. Knowledge is often not enough – we have to work on attitudes and perceptions, as it is these things that drive behaviour.

Behaviour is normally the result of a decision-making process. Decisions are made based on a wide variety of criteria – some seemingly logical, others, totally illogical. The criteria include:

- knowledge

- prejudice

- psychological make-up

- event specific conditions (the weather, the time and so on).

Many observers, when analysing behaviour, respond to certain actions with questions such as 'Why the hell did he do that?' A variety of these issues are discussed in Chapter 1 in the section called 'The Psychology of Risk, or Why Do People Do Stupid Things?'. Many of the behaviours we don't want to see happen are in fact predictable, but only if you take the time to analyse and understand how people come to make decisions.

Part of this analysis should concentrate on how people perceive risk. Perception forms a basic part of prejudice, and distorts knowledge. Chapter 1 discusses the issues relating to risk perception in depth, but it's worth outlining some of them at this point.

If things are unfamiliar, outside your control and imposed upon you, they are automatically perceived as more risky than something that is known, in your hands and performed by you personally. This perception drives decision making on risk to such an extent that it has led to inappropriate risk management investment decisions. These inappropriate decisions waste time and money without addressing real risk efficiently or effectively. They have also led to the reduction of the credibility of information security as a practice, which in turn has lead to ongoing future problems obtaining reasonable investment to meet real risks. Examples of such inappropriate investment occur often. Most competently built e-commerce systems have extensive, expensive technology protecting them from external attack. This technology includes firewalls, complex cryptographic facilities and intrusion detection systems (IDS). Whilst these are necessary, not least to ensure basic legal and financial principles such as non-repudiation, there is often a parallel *lack* of investment in staff training, HR recruitment procedures and management control over contractors and similar short-term employees.

A further issue in dealing with inappropriate behaviour (in the context of how risk is perceived) is that of *how* to meet awareness needs. I have already asserted that awareness is more than publicity and giveaways (mouse mats, fluffy stick-on bugs, pens, drinks mats and so on, collectively known as 'collateral'). You need to identify those behaviours you want (or don't want), and then try to initiate (or stop) them. If these things are identified, then it becomes easier to focus one's effort – indeed, it becomes possible to operate by setting measurable objectives. Such a technique forms the core of Part 2 of this book.

Having hopefully provided you with a way of taking awareness forward, I have also looked at another matter – that of how information security professionals and/or practitioners (in many circumstances there is a difference) are perceived. This perception drives many prejudices, which in turn affects the way security investment decisions are made. We have to address our own image – mainly because it has become tarnished.

## WHY AWARENESS?

Raising awareness is the single most effective thing an information security practitioner can do to make a positive difference to their organization.

> *The idea is the more lines of defense a company has in place, the less likely there will be a successful penetration, the more chance there is that an attack can be detected and the most likeliness an attacker will give up and move on to another more vulnerable target. In this light, many people might think of multiple layers of technology such as firewalls, networks, host and network intrusion detection systems, bastion hosts, and so on that would comprise this defense of depth. However, we know based on published surveys and analyses that the biggest threat to our technology environment is often ourselves.*

> *Organizations that want to survive in the coming years need to develop a comprehensive approach to information security, embracing both the human and technical dimensions. They also need to properly fund, train, staff and empower those tasked with enterprise-wide information security.*

*In addition, human error is often the root cause of problems in some of the most sophisticated technological implementations. This is why security awareness in your company is so critical.*[2]

*Security apathy and ignorance are the biggest threats to computer systems. . . . And the best way to achieve a significant and lasting improvement in computer security is not by throwing more technical solutions at the problem – it's by raising awareness and training and educating all computer users in the basics of computer security.*[3]

Too often awareness campaigns are run by people who are incompetent. They are incompetent not because they are fools or are lazy – incompetence occurs when you step outside the envelope of your own capability. I am an incompetent flute player but a competent guitarist. I was a competent (although never skilful) rugby player, but remain absolutely useless at golf.

Awareness for most information security practitioners is that small part of information security practice that they feel they have to do because someone has told them it's worthwhile – and anyway, BS 7799 says they should do it. So the temptation is to try and run a campaign using your own current skills – and incompetence strikes.

This book aims at reducing your incompetence gap. Perhaps the most chilling quotation comes from the notorious convicted hacker Kevin Mitnick:

*... the human side of computer security is easily exploited and constantly overlooked. Companies spend millions of dollars on firewalls, encryption and secure access devices, and it's money wasted, because none of these measures address the weakest link in the security chain.*

Kevin Mitnick – hacker

You only have to read Mitnick's material on 'social engineering' to understand fully what he means.

---

2   SANS reading room material. Article: 'The Ultimate Defense of Depth: Security Awareness in Your Company', Brian D. Voss, 11 August, 2001.
3   Native Intelligence, Inc. 2000 – http://nativeintelligence.com/index.aspx.

# THE RATIONALE FOR SECURITY AWARENESS

## STATISTICS

Statistics on the number and percentage of security incidents generated from inside an organization suggest that internal users are responsible for at least around 70 per cent, and that most of these incidents are the result of user error, mishap and ignorance. The statistics have remained reasonably consistent over a number of years. Many of these incidents could have been prevented by improved understanding and by changes in attitude to information security. Losses from information security incidents have been estimated as being up to 3 per cent[4] of corporate annual profit, the effect of substantially reducing them could be immense.

The UK Government Department of Trade and Industry (DTI) Information Security Breaches Survey 2004 makes five high-level recommendations, of which the second states:

> *Integrate security into normal business practice, through a clear security policy and staff education.*

One of the key findings of the 2003 Computer Security Institute (CSI)/FBI Computer Crime and Security Survey was:

> *As in previous years, virus incidents (82 per cent) and insider abuse of network access (80 per cent) were the most cited forms of attack or abuse.*

The CSI/FBI Survey also reckoned that the biggest costs were associated with viruses, laptop theft and Internet abuse. All of these issues can be addressed positively through sound education and awareness.

In recent years there has been a swing in various surveys towards external attack; the numbers seem to be indicating that external criminality is increasing. Much of this change has been due to the increase in Internet connectivity, and that it is now relatively easy to detect (although perhaps not so easy to prevent) events impacting on outward-facing computer systems. This will lead to increased numbers of detected incidents generated externally. Many of these are small scale, and only recorded because they were external, and because they are easy to detect. See the 'Perception of Risk' section in Chapter 1 to find out why these externally generated events are often seen as more important than internally generated ones.

---

4    ISF Information Security Survey Analysis (1998).

The statistics further suggest that some 55–70 per cent of incidents are the result of insiders making mistakes – either through ignorance or stupidity. Bearing in mind the fact that some 2–3 per cent of profit[5] is potentially lost due to information security incidents, the potential for making a significant contribution to your organization is very great.

It is important to remember that the most effective security countermeasure is a balance of controls. You need a sound technical infrastructure – that is undeniable. You need sound internal governance. You need appropriate measures to deal with Corporate Governance. You need workable internal processes to deal with new people joining your organization, just as you need sound processes for dealing with leavers. This notwithstanding, you need measures to reduce the number of errors, and to rectify the damage caused by the incurably stupid.

## STANDARDS

There are a number of drivers (other than common sense and statistics) that make pursuing security awareness very worthwhile. These include a number of international standards, although there is no single specific public standard published at present that defines security awareness practice.

### *OECD*

The Organization for Economic Co-operation and Development's (OECD) *Guidelines for the Security of Information Systems and Networks – Towards a culture of security* published in 2002 outline a series of nine principles. Awareness is the first of the nine, which states:

1.  *Awareness*

    *Participants should be aware of the need for security of information systems and networks and what they can do to enhance security.*

    *Awareness of the risks and available safeguards is the first line of defence for the security of information systems and networks. Information systems and networks can be affected by both internal and external risks. Participants should understand that security failures may significantly harm systems and networks under their control.*

    *They should also be aware of the potential harm to others arising from interconnectivity and interdependency. Participants should be*

---

5    Information Security Forum - Information Security Survey Analysis (1998).

*aware of the configuration of, and available updates for, their system, its place within networks, good practices that they can implement to enhance security, and the needs of other participants.*

The other eight principles are:

2. *Responsibility – All participants are responsible for the security of information systems and networks.*

3. *Response – Participants should act in a timely and co-operative manner to prevent, detect and respond to security incidents.*

4. *Ethics – Participants should respect the legitimate interests of others.*

5. *Democracy – The security of information systems and networks should be compatible with essential values of a democratic society.*

6. *Risk assessment – Participants should conduct risk assessments.*

7. *Security design and implementation – Participants should incorporate security as an essential element of information systems and networks.*

8. *Security management – Participants should adopt a comprehensive approach to security management.*

9. *Reassessment – Participants should review and reassess the security of information systems and networks, and make appropriate modifications to security policies, practices, measures and procedures.*

The emphasis on awareness (particularly as it is the first of the nine) is strong. The other principles are fundamental, and this enhances the OECD view that awareness is extremely important.

## Information Security Forum (ISF)

The Information Security Forum (ISF) is a member-based organization that draws membership from large organizations across the world. Most of its work and output is retained for member use only, but it has decided to publish the Standard of Good Practice (SOGP), a thorough set of control statements for information security. The SOGP states the following (in section SM24 Security Awareness):

*Awareness of information security should be maintained via effective awareness programmes covering all individuals with access to information or systems within the enterprise. Employees (including contractors) should be provided with guidance to help them understand information security, the importance of complying with policies/ standards and to be aware of their own personal responsibilities.*

*Formal awareness programmes should be:*

- *coordinated by a designated individual or group run using structured education/training programmes and specialized awareness material supported by top management;*

- *kept up to date with current practices;*

- *applied to all individuals with access to information or systems.*

*The level of awareness within the enterprise should be measured and reviewed periodically.*

The SOGP also states:

*Education/training should be provided to all personnel with control over, or access to, the organization's information and systems. This should equip all personnel with the know-how required to assess security requirements, propose security controls and ensure controls function effectively*

*Education/training should also be provided to ensure that:*

- *business users use systems correctly and apply security controls;*

- *IT staff develop systems in a disciplined manner and run installations or communications networks correctly;*

- *information security specialists understand the business, know how to run security projects and can communicate effectively.*

## ISACA/COBIT

COBIT (the Control Objectives for IT) from ISACA (Information Systems Audit and Control Association), have made awareness one of the six main guidelines of their control framework.

## ISO 13335

Part Three of ISO/IEC TR 13335, a standard often referred to as GMITS (Guidance for the Management of IT Security), contains excellent guidance to a number of information security practices, including awareness.

## BS 7799

The mostly widely used information security standard, BS 7799 says in Section 8.2.2:

> *Information security awareness, education and training*
>
> *All employees and the organization and, where relevant, contractors and third party users should receive appropriate awareness training and regular updates in organizational policies and procedures, as relevant to their job function.*

The standard also states that such initiatives should be ongoing and suitable to the roles and responsibilities of the people concerned.

### Summary of standards

All these extracts from these various standards make a clear point; security awareness is a fundamental requirement if one is to even contemplate meeting best practice. Given that many industries (financial services for example) are driven by regulation, and that this regulation strongly recommends adherence to standards, in many circumstances security awareness is a prescribed requirement.

The Financial Services Authority (FSA) in the UK has strongly suggested that certification to BS 7799 is seen as meeting many of their regulatory requirements that relate to information security.

## PARALLEL ACTIVITIES

Awareness is not a panacea; panaceas for information security do not exist. To make awareness effective, it is a given that other parallel activities have to take place if you are to succeed. The most important of these include:

## DESIGNING OUT ERROR

It makes sense to idiot-proof your systems and processes. Take for example the electric plug used in the UK. You can't insert it in the socket the wrong way round. This book does not teach you how to design out error – I can merely tell you that by doing so you reduce risk.

Designing out error should start with the obvious.[6] I have heard it suggested that the act of performing standard risk analysis on any system reduces risk without any formal intervention or action by the security practitioner. This may seem improbable, but the fact remains that risk is reduced simply because the person interviewed as part of the analysis exercise realizes just where the yawning gaps are in their control infrastructure, and puts them right immediately as part of business as usual. These control improvements are initially invisible to the security folk. The improvements form part of designing out error.

A well-designed system is normally a more secure system. A process developed by a high quality project management regime incorporates better controls and security practice. This is often because sound project management includes a risk analysis phase and it often communicates with those people most likely to be affected by the project – the poor users of the resulting system. They are by far the best qualified to design a set of controls, and are more familiar with the real risks that affect their work.

## TRAINING

If your people aren't trained, it should come as no surprise if they make mistakes. If there's one thing you can do to assist your operations staff it is good training. Let them know what they are to do, and let them know what's expected of them. Very few people know what their responsibilities actually are. Good training reduces error. Good training improves security because it reduces the error count. If people know what's expected of them, they'll normally carry it out.

Chapter 4 contains extensive discussion and analysis on training and how it relates to security awareness. It is a powerful tool that you need to take account of when initiating an awareness programme.

## TECHNICAL MATTERS

Information security grew out of the IT profession. Many practitioners have a technical background (although this is changing). This legacy has led to a distinct technical bias to the profession. When you rely on one single control (or type of control) you can become exposed to risks that are not covered (see 'The Maginot Line Syndrome' and 'The Potato Syndrome' overleaf).

---

6    Sometimes known as the 'bleeding obvious' by Basil Fawlty – the character played by John
     Cleese in *Fawlty Towers*.

## The Maginot Line Syndrome

After the Armistice in 1918, the French government were determined that the despoiling of their northern regions would never happen again. They remained highly suspicious of the Germans (with hindsight, they were right to remain so), and decided that they should protect themselves using their undoubted engineering and planning skills. Thus the Maginot Line was born. It was an extremely long, almost continuous chain of banks, ditches, gun emplacements and obstacles. It ran the length of the Franco-German border. It was organized to provide 'killing zones' of the most horrendous nature. It was a formidable undertaking, and a frightening obstacle. The Germans dealt with it by invading France via Belgium. The rest is history. Never rely on a single line of defence.

## The Potato Syndrome

There is no one single solution. Relying on a single thing creates a potential single point of failure. Consider the humble potato. The potato provides the highest food value of any crop. It grows well in a variety of climates. It was so effective that entire parts of the world came to depend on it completely. This had advantages: the land supported more people than before, and starvation became less of a problem. Potato eaters often enjoyed better health than those on other diets.

Unfortunately the potato has a rather critical weakness – potato blight. Historically, in areas that depended solely on potatoes, when blight destroyed the crop, there was mass starvation.

If you rely on a single thing, you are open to potential catastrophic failure. Remember the potato – it has a lot to teach us.

You need a strong technical infrastructure – populated with appropriate tools. At the time of going to press such tools might include (in no particular order):

* access control facilities
* anti-virus software

- browsing controls

- e-mail filters

- event logging and monitoring capability

- firewall deployment

- intrusion detection.

There will no doubt be additions to the above list. To make awareness effective, you need to make the most of your technical controls.

Therefore, you need a combination of things to survive, just as you need a balanced combination of controls to address information security issues. To rely totally on technical controls is foolhardy.

## MANAGEMENT

A sound management structure is needed to implement information security effectively.

Management is a very broad subject, but let me place it in some form of context. The subjects need to be covered include:

- internal governance (policy, standards, procedures and so on)

- intelligence (management information, including event logs, monitoring information and suchlike)

- education, training and awareness (ETA)

- risk management (including project based risk analysis)

- audit and compliance.

### Internal governance

Without the rulebook that is internal governance, you will find it extremely hard to operate, particularly in complex organizations. Figure 1.1 outlines the sort of policies most information security practitioners would expect to influence.

Not all the published documents are written in the same manner or in the same style. It is established wisdom that the higher documents (policy and sub-policies) are reviewed occasionally (perhaps six-monthly or annually), but due to their relatively generic nature, and the fact that they often have to

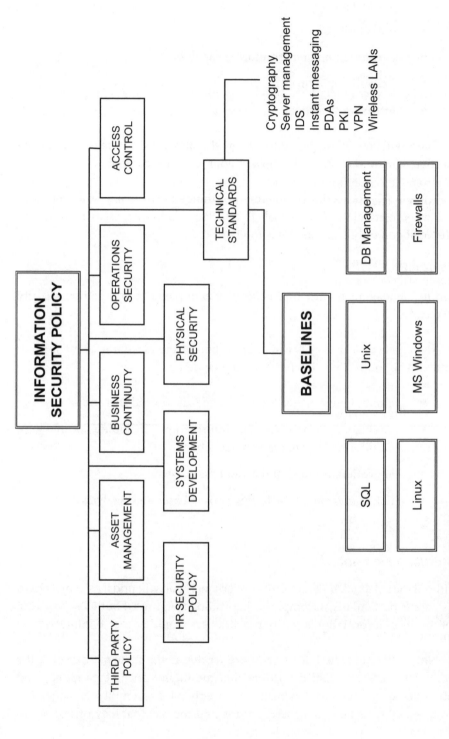

**Figure 1.1    Policy and standards hierarchy**

be periodically revisited and authorized by very busy people, they tend to be fairly static in content.

Other documents are much more volatile, and require revisiting on a more regular basis. This is especially so of documents that provide specific technical guidance (such as the baseline guides to the building of secure server platforms illustrated above), as they tend to change whenever new technical vulnerabilities are uncovered. This can occur more than once a day.

There are many other documents that need to be put in place in an operational environment. Many of these are low level, covering processes and procedures. These have been omitted from the diagram for the sake of clarity.

## Intelligence

In order to maintain the 'manage by fact'[7] principle (a concept expanded upon in Chapter 4), you need to make use of trustworthy intelligence. Such intelligence feeds come from:

- access control software

- conversations in the pub

- direct reports from co-workers

- firewall logs

- helpdesk event logs

- incident management procedures

- intrusion detection systems (IDS)

- system audit trails

- system control files.

Some security managers take multiple feeds and use them to create 'dashboards'. These are reports that indicate the status of devices, processes, controls and so on, using a RAG (red, amber, green) marker. Such reporting concepts can be used either for compliance checking (for example, indicating whether devices are built to specified company standards), or for indicating event status.

---

7    Managing by fact is the opposite of what usually happens. Most people manage by 'myth',
     conjecture, bias and guesswork.

If your security management information is missing or untrustworthy, you will not be able to provide reasonable assurance that your company is meeting policy, and thereby failing to reduce the potential for harm.

## Risk management

Risk management means the practice of identifying, qualifying and controlling information risk as it affects an organization.

The process normally involves a practice called 'risk analysis'; a formal process that often makes use of commercial methodologies (such as CRAMM, the UK Government approved method). There are others, including SARA/Sprint (from the Information Security Forum). The methods are built around a series of steps that include:

- impact analysis – calculation of the effects of an incident. This is normally expressed, but not in every case, in financial terms;

- risk assessment – estimation of the likelihood of an incident;

- control selection – a process to meet risks by avoiding, minimising, accepting or transferring them. Transferring risk normally involves the purchasing of appropriate insurance.

Risk analysis can also be less rigid, and use informal methods. What is clear is that these processes help practitioners focus on those potential events that are likely to cause the biggest problems. If you are not performing some form of risk management, your awareness initiatives will be considerably less effective. Risk analysis can be project based or part of an established systems development lifecycle (SDLC).

## Audit and compliance

If your organization does not have a solid audit and compliance regime, awareness will be less effective.

## SUMMARY

This book is not designed to help you become an all-round information security manager. That is why the previous few sections have been brief, and the list of potential parallel activities is probably incomplete. However, without them, security awareness would be much less effective. One of the main elements of a control infrastructure is balance. Too much emphasis on a single element and you're likely to face a problem.

# HOW IDIOTIC?

A considerable percentage of security incidents are down to errors. Many of these errors are a result of ignorance, which should normally be addressed by training. Other errors are simply down to stupidity. These can be addressed by such practices as designing out errors, but many cannot be legislated for. The 'Piltdown Man Syndrome' section below illustrates how human foibles can cause people to make big mistakes.

## PILTDOWN MAN SYNDROME

The now mythic Piltdown Man is one of the most famous frauds in the history of palaeontology. In 1912 Charles Dawson discovered an apparently hominid skull and related jawbone in a quarry near Piltdown, Sussex, England. For many years palaeontologists had assumed the existence of a human ancestor who linked modern humans with more primitive ape-like relations. Finding this 'missing link' became the stated goal of many field palaeontologists. The bones unearthed by Dawson appeared to be the expected missing link, a mixture of human and ape, with the noble brow of *Homo sapiens* and a primitive jaw.

As with most scientific breakthroughs, you have to consider context and perspective. In 1912, the UK and Germany were locked in a terrifying arms race. Rivalry in all fields was huge, and any opportunity to beat and belittle the other was taken. In human palaeontology, the Germans had the upper hand. In 1856 the first Neanderthal fossil discovery was made in Germany. In the next 50 years finds were made in continental Europe and in Asia. Not in Britain. Given the animosity between Germany and the UK at the time, there was a perceived need for a British win. So, in 1912, the fossil remains of an ancient Pleistocene hominid found in the Piltdown quarries became fêted in London (although not in Paris or Berlin). During the years 1912 to 1915 the Piltdown quarries yielded (from the same stratified context) more skulls, a canine tooth, another jawbone, a tool carved from an elephant tusk, and fossil teeth from a number of Pleistocene animals.

Unsurprisingly, initial reaction to the finds was variable. British palaeontologists were enthusiastic; the French and American palaeontologists tended to be sceptical. The objectors held that the initial discoveries of a jawbone and skull were obviously from two different animals, and that their discovery together was simply an accident of placement. The report of the discovery of the second skull converted many of the sceptics; one accident of placement was plausible, two were not.

The hoax was revealed as a deliberate fraud as late as 1953 (41 years later)! The first skull was eventually dated as medieval, as was the second. The jawbone was from an orang-utan, whilst the other fossils were genuine, but from (probably) Tunisia, Malta and Central Africa. The bones had been deliberately aged using simple staining agents.

The fraud was successful because:

- the team finding the specimens had excellent credentials;
- some of the experts were incompetent;
- primitive analytical tools were used;
- the forgery was skilfully implemented;
- it matched what was expected from theory.

It is the final characteristic of this example that is important. When information, behaviour or evidence correspond to our expectations, we are likely to assume they are correct. Remember the old saying: 'In any collection of data, the figure that is obviously correct, beyond all need of checking, is the mistake.'

Let's relate this characteristic to information security.

## SECURITY MANAGER'S ASSUMPTIONS

A former colleague who had a problem called me one day. An apparently deliberate attempt was being made to hack into his organization's network. Initial analysis showed that at some point after a new user account was set up, an attempt was made to illegally access that user account. An automatic log record print out listed each of these illegal access attempts.

There was no geographic or chronological pattern to these attacks. Whoever was attacking knew exactly when a new user account was being set up, no matter where the user was based (it was a global network). Meetings were held, and no information was passed other than in neutral premises, avoiding the use of phones, mobiles, fax and e-mail. This clandestine approach was tiresome, inefficient but considered necessary. Still, the hacker ploughed on, testing the new accounts whenever they were created.

A very sophisticated sniffer device was placed on the network, tasked with looking for unauthorized devices. It was placed in a physically secure location, without permission from anyone other than those involved in the project. A number of trips were taken to overseas locations, investigating rumours and checking out what were fruitless leads. There was no evidence, no joy and no luck.

Eventually, a test network was set up, remote from any external connection. This was to test the next generation of sniffers. As the system was populated with dummy user accounts, the hacker struck. The system log detected him trying to access the new dummy accounts. Given that the test network was in a single room, with no external connectivity, the hacker had to be something else. Just as the palaeontologists assessing the Piltdown Man finds had leaped on the missing link, the security managers had assumed that the alert log messages were genuine (because a classic hacking technique is to target new accounts, looking for default passwords and the like). They weren't. There was a bug in the network operating system. It has since been corrected.

Stories of user stupidity are legion. I have heard of people folding a paper message in half prior to faxing it 'to keep it safe' – regardless of the fact that the recipient saw a facsimile of a blank folded sheet of paper.

## ATMs AND STUPIDITY

Another example of stupidity involves a major UK retail bank. The incident happened at a time when ATMs (Automated Teller Machines) were extremely important to people who wanted to make large purchases. This was because credit card penetration was much lower than now, and the banks limited cheques to small amounts. Just about the only way to make purchases above £50 was to get cash out of the ATM.

The golden hour of 12:00 to 13:00 on Christmas Eve is the time when many men do their Christmas shopping. In this incident, such shoppers were out in force, and the ATM networks were taking a hammering. So much so that the operators in the computer room at the bank in question noticed that some devices (especially the customized computers used to check ATM user PINs) were beginning to hit capacity. These devices (often referred to as hardware security modules or HSMs) could, when being thrashed by massive throughput, start to heat up. In this incident, one (of three) was getting very warm, and was probably causing (or at least, likely to cause) a bottleneck, and could have reduced ATM service levels.

One operator had an idea. He had been working on a concept that is close to what is now known as 'load balancing'. He decided that he could ease the pressure on the HSMs by running a program that would balance the load between all three. He ran the program, and the whole system went down immediately, and remained down for six hours.

There are many lessons to be learned from this event, but the following year, the same person (who for reasons unknown had kept his job), when asked about the event, said 'Yea. It was I. All I did was this....' He then proceeded to do exactly the same thing, with the same results. He did not stay in the post long afterwards. You cannot legislate for this type of person, and you cannot legislate for a management system that allows operators to update live systems in such a way.

## WHY DO ACCIDENTS HAPPEN?

My father always used to paraphrase Freud and tell me that 'There's no such thing as an accident.' Freud's interpretation of accidents is largely based on the premise that we subconsciously allow things to happen and consciously declare them to be accidental.

You may not be totally convinced by Freud, but there is no doubt that accidents are often the result of subconscious activity. There are myriad examples of people making mistakes even in circumstances designed to reduce the chances of error. Experts make errors all the time. Most transport accidents are due, in some degree or other, to driver or pilot error. If you think you would never allow your attention to waver in such circumstances, please consider the following question:

> Have you ever driven a car and arrived safely at your destination, and then realized that there were parts of the journey of which you have no memory whatsoever?

Experienced drivers are 'unconsciously competent' which allows them to concentrate on other things (their tax bill, the song on the radio or last night's curry) rather than the immediate process of driving a vehicle. It's when you are in this state that accidents happen.

Norman F Dixon, Professor of Psychology, University College London suggests another reason we act irrationally and cause accidents is because our in-built survival mechanisms kick in, in situations for which they were not designed.

---

**Survival Mechanisms Working Too Well**

In an aircraft crash the pilots became distracted by an important, but not necessarily fatal, event. A warning signal had triggered telling them that the aircraft's front wheel had not locked itself into place for landing. The pilots spent some time trying to force the wheel down (even manually) and were so engrossed in the task that they failed to hear other alarms (such as the ground proximity alert). The plane crashed, killing all on board. The human survival mechanism that kicked in focuses nearly all attention on threatening situations. This is useful if confronted by a predator or an enemy, but actually is sometimes counterproductive in an aircraft cockpit. The pilots focused on the wheel lock alert, and in doing so actually blocked out other (more urgent) alerts.

The world is full of examples of people being presented with alarms and alerts, and ignoring them assuming that there's been an alert error or malfunction. If your fire alarm keeps going off, it's hard to persuade people to evacuate the building each time it does. At some point, there will be a real fire.

## SUMMARY

Information security awareness is a fundamental part of effective security management. It is not a panacea and requires competence and attention to be paid to a number of parallel activities. These include:

- empowering policies and standards;

- providing a sound technical infrastructure;

- helping ensure staff are competent in their main jobs;

- enabling an effective systems and process design environment.

People make mistakes and can sometimes be stupid. You have to recognize this rather than pretend it doesn't happen. This statement is neither malicious nor condescending – it is a statement of fact meant to make your task clearer. Once you recognize that we are all capable of making mistakes, you will be more able to try and help your organization avoid, reduce or transfer the impact of unwanted events.

The majority of errors, security incidents and disasters have, as part of their foundation, an assumption. This assumption is normally a variant on 'it'll never happen to me'.

Remember that even the most experienced of professionals can make errors of epic proportions. Never assume that staff of great experience and competence cannot be subject to human foibles – they are and will continue to be.

# PART 1

# A Framework for Understanding

# CHAPTER 1

# Employee Risk

## PERCEPTION OF RISK

Most people react to risk in an emotional manner. This reaction often comes as a surprise to people who understand the true statistics relating to risk.

Sarah Hogg, chairman of Frontier Economics published an article in the *Independent* newspaper. Her article discussed the problems occurring in the UK rail network:

> On my way to a train that runs at less than half the speed it did a few weeks ago, I drive past a sign telling me that 61 people have died on Lincolnshire's roads this year so far. Some 449 have been seriously injured. Thus, in our part of the world, are the police illustrating a truth ignored in the aftermath of the Hatfield crash? Cars kill more people than trains…

Yet because we perceive train-based risk in a way that is different from road (car)-based risk, we spend somewhere in the region of 150 times more on train safety than car safety per life lost.

There are other examples of the effect of risk perception. In healthcare, a great deal of money is spent on treating diseases like cancer. This is undoubtedly welcome, but more lives would be saved if appropriate resources were spent on controlling post-operative infections and the spread of infective agents such as MRSA. These 'appropriate resources' would be significantly less than the sums currently allocated to combat certain diseases. The reasons for this disparity relate less to clinical logic than public relations, culture and risk perception.

In organizations such as government-funded healthcare, local government and other public services, the attitude to risk management is often clouded by a perceived public need for certainty. Nothing is ever 100 per cent, just as no information system is 100 per cent secure. This absolutist attitude makes managing risk in certain sectors more complex than it need be. In politics, risk management is often based more on managing public opinion than dealing with the reality of the risks faced.

There is an information source in the US called the Vanderbilt University Television News Index and Abstracts. This was on one occasion used to perform content analysis of news coverage from January 1984 to February 1986. The research looked at over 500 evening news broadcasts, and discovered that some 1.7 per cent of the news time reflected environmental risks. During the same period, 57 stories discussed tobacco, whilst 482 concerned accidents and safety in the airline industry. Based on the number of actual deaths, there should be 26.5 minutes of coverage regarding tobacco for every *second* of airline accidents. For the most part, the ratio of acute to chronic deaths, in terms of network coverage, runs at about 7 to 1 (see below for more on chronic and acute risks).

Furthermore, it became very apparent that news stories tend to reflect the location of the television network news bureaus rather than the actual impact of the events themselves. In the US example given above, 'peripheral' states such as Alabama and West Virginia received about a third the amount of coverage as California and New York based on the number of incidents. Guess where the news bureaus are located!

John Allen Paulos, Professor of Mathematics at Temple University in Philadelphia, describes the ongoing public lack of understanding of numbers and risk in his seminal work *Innumeracy – Mathematical illiteracy and its consequences*. Amongst the many issues he debates, he outlines how people 'personalize' events, forgetting that sometimes bad things just occur, that events do not run in threes, and that the adage 'shit happens' is true. The link between innumeracy and 'pseudoscience' is one of Allen's strongest themes. If we actually thought about things rationally, stock market scams, pyramid selling and fortune tellers would become a thing of the past. If we actually thought about things rationally, risk perception would be less of a problem.

A strong factor in risk perception relates to control. Risk perception is more than statistics. If a threat is external and 'exotic' (that is, unfamiliar and perhaps strange), and if the person perceiving the risk feels they are not in control of a situation, the perception of risk is higher. For example, if you were to attend a late night party some way distant from your home, and then decide you want to leave, most people (providing they haven't been drinking) would think driving home to be safer than walking across town late at night. Fear of mugging and assault drives many people (particularly women) into their cars. The truth is that driving a car, at any time, is about the most dangerous thing an adult can do in the UK. The fact that mugging is an external threat makes it more threatening.

Table 1.1 shows how some perception can distort risk.[1]

**Table 1.1    Risk perception**

| Less risky | More risky |
|---|---|
| Chronic | Acute |
| Controllable | Uncontrollable |
| Controlled by self | Controlled by others |
| Detectable | Undetectable |
| Diffuse in time and space | Focused in time and space |
| Fair | Unfair |
| Familiar | Unfamiliar |
| Immediate | Delayed |
| Natural | Artificial |
| Voluntary | Involuntary |

## CHRONIC – ACUTE

If a medical condition is chronic (that is, a condition that has built up over time, such as heart disease or diabetes), it is less dramatic and is not perceived in the same way as an acute condition (a condition that is sudden, such as infection by the Ebola virus or a car crash). If all the 10 000 people who die prematurely each year in the UK from smoking-related illnesses were to do so at one o'clock in the afternoon on 10 February in Parliament Square, the reaction would be very negative, and rapid remedial action would follow. The fact that most smoking-related deaths are attributable to chronic conditions, and that each death tends to be diffuse in time and space, lessens their impact. Each death is a tragedy, but doesn't get a mention in the media other than when the victim is famous.

The major medical killers are chronic. Acute deaths get the headlines.

In information security, chronic issues normally relate to structural and infrastructural issues, such as poor systems design, inadequate procedures or badly trained staff. These are difficult to deal with for a number of reasons; not least that admitting their existence could suggest someone in the organization is to blame. Never underestimate the power of personal embarrassment!

The issues of chronic and acute conditions can be applied to information security quite readily. People tend to focus on acute issues (especially if they are perceived as being 'external', 'alien' or 'controlled by others'). Such issues include computer virus infection, hacking and industrial espionage. A specific

---

1    Fischhoff B., Slovic P., and Lichtenstein S., 'Weighing the Risks', *Environment*, 21 (1979).

example of chronic risk is the degree of trust many companies place on individuals who have developed systems from scratch.

I have seen many examples of people who have acted as designer, programmer, operator and maintainer of a business-critical application. In no instance had the person provided any meaningful documentation. The organizations had exposed themselves to considerable risk. Should the person leave, go sick or die the business-critical application would be without support and could fail catastrophically. Furthermore, the person who developed and maintained the application was in a position to defraud the company by a number of means. These ranged from straightforward embezzlement to blackmail. The risk this person represented was chronic rather than acute. In many instances the organizations decided to ignore the risk on the grounds that they did not want to offend the person involved. The acceptance of such profound risk would not be countenanced if the risk had been perceived as external to the organization.

## Moral outrage

One of the most public illustrations of how risk is perceived and reacted to is called 'moral outrage' by sociologists and psychologists. This syndrome is well understood by the UK newspaper industry – some newspapers are keen to develop such outrage – normally to score political points or increase their circulation. They focus mostly on health issues, such as BSE and the MMR triple vaccine.

The example of the MMR (Mumps, Measles and Rubella) vaccine is particularly poignant. There was a report published in the UK that suggested there was a link between the MMR jab and autism in young children. The research was based around findings of various antibodies in the guts of autistic children. The report unleashed a plethora of stories (many heartbreaking) of children becoming autistic after having the vaccine. The result was a significant fall in the numbers of children being vaccinated. This pattern has remained, despite numerous later reports totally refuting the original research. The original results were held up to particular scepticism as it was apparently sponsored by an organization that had a vested interest in the matter. The numbers of children missing out on the jab created the potential conditions for an epidemic of the diseases MMR was designed to protect against. The projected numbers of deaths and instances of severe side-effects from these diseases are many times greater than the potential numbers of children who may (even in the original research) have been afflicted with autism. The moral outrage has had a real effect, and could have disastrous consequences for many children in the near future.

The subject in question can become the centre of a 'scare', and is often met by a 'campaign' (normally run on behalf of a supposedly silent majority by an extremely vocal minority). What is plain is that the matter is often treated to attention that exceeds any real risk or threat. The phenomenon can result in a change in word association; in the UK for example, note how an asylum seeker, rather than being a pitied, oppressed person fleeing despotism, is now perceived by many as a deceptive sponger looking for an easy ride.

Information security suffers from similar spates of outrage. The overblown reputations of Bulgarian virus writers, script kiddies, Fluffy Bunny and the Cult of the Dead Cow (two hacker organizations) are testament to the phenomenon. A famous example from Australia centres round a real hacking event that impacted on an electricity supply company. The hacking event received 10 times the press coverage of a later event that was caused by a cormorant landing on some power lines. The damage caused by the cormorant cost between 20 and 30 times that caused by the hacker. As the first event was externally imposed rather than an act of nature, it was seen as outrageous.

We continue to see similar outrage about phantom withdrawals from bank ATMs, despite the fact that nearly every such event is a mistake by the cardholder, or a minor fraud perpetrated by a member of the cardholder's family. We hear ludicrous questions from vapid television journalists such as 'Is the Internet safe?' when there has been a spate of fraud. The fact is, time and money is spent dealing with perceived risks during outbreaks of outrage, and this is normally greater than that required when the real levels of risk are used as the basis of decision making. Avoid being swept up by such rumours. And don't start any. And beware of cormorants.

Information security is as subject to the whims of fashion as any other subject, and the concept of moral outrage can manifest because of this. Fashions affect solutions as well as threats. Public key infrastructure (PKI) was touted as the ideal solution for all security matters for many years. Note the quote below from Carl Ellison and Bruce Schneier 's article 'What you're not being told about Public Key Infrastructure' (*Computer Security Journal*, 16/1, 2000):

> *Computer security has been victim of the 'year of the...' syndrome. First it was firewalls, then intrusion detection systems, then VPNs, and now certification authorities (CAs) and public key infrastructure.*

*'If you only buy X' the sales pitch goes, 'then you will be secure.' But reality is never that simple, and that is especially true with PKI.*

I can recall too many similar magic bullets. At one point, smartcards were going to save the world. This went on for about 15 years before somebody actually provided a smartcard solution that somebody was prepared to pay for. Time, effort and money will be expended on fashionable causes (including awareness). Avoid the hype, save your money and stick to what's actually important!

## DIFFUSE IN TIME AND SPACE – FOCUSED IN TIME AND SPACE

The practice of business continuity has an element within it referred to as 'disaster recovery'. Planning for disasters makes sense, as disasters do happen. The oft-quoted 'plane lands on a building' scenario, once derided as an extreme example, is now too familiar after 9/11. Indeed, the British Midland 737 crash at East Midlands Airport in 1989 near Kegworth in the UK almost took out a major clearing bank's data centre as well as killing 46 people on board.

It is easy to focus on disasters, but I believe that there is scope for considerable damage from events that are truly 'diffuse in time and space'. An example of such an event would be an error in the monthly calculation of bonuses in a 25-year life insurance policy. Each event is small, but the error is compounded over time. Because these events are often small, they are often unreported. As they are unreported, they are not costed. As they are not costed, few people know that they've happened. The cumulative effect could, however, be very high.

Another example is the consistent but undetected failure of a backup procedure designed to protect a large database. Each small failure would have negligible effect. The accumulation of error could be devastating should there be a need to restore the database fully from backup. The event that creates the need for the restoration could be acute, such as a flood; the damage really comes as a result of the chronic backup failure.

An example of a diffuse event is that of disk crashes on laptops. Local stores (held on laptops) of information are rarely backed up. Such events, especially across large mobile workforces, are difficult to measure, and they represent a significant risk for information. Laptops are also prone to theft; not only do you have the potential for direct loss (a decent laptop costs over £2000), there is also information loss and the cost of recovery. This issue will increase in significance as PDAs and similar technology become more widespread. One figure cited in

2004 for an organization of about 25 000 staff in the UK is a loss of £1 million per annum due to theft/loss of laptops. This figure was for hardware only. The overall problem had never been addressed because each loss was seen only in the context of the department from which it had been lost or stolen. It was only when someone added up the numbers that the true extent of losses was realized and the problem dealt with. This was done by:

- centralizing purchasing (gaining significant reductions in purchase price into the bargain);

- creating a hardware register;

- making staff responsible for equipment in their care (and telling them what these responsibilities entailed);

- making people sign personally for their equipment on receipt;

- marking each piece with ultra-violet ink indicating ownership;

- sticking labels onto the laptops stating 'This belongs to XXX Corp Asset Number nnn'.

## FAMILIAR – UNFAMILIAR

Familiarity breeds contempt. But how often have you undertaken a task that seemed formidable, and then reported how easy it was afterward; and realized that your anxiety centred on the fact that you had never done the task before? The same principle occurs in risk perception. We fear hackers. We don't fear the guys we know well in the IT support department. Such fear is innate, inbuilt and totally understandable. The downside of this survival mechanism (most innate emotions and feelings can be traced back to inbuilt survival mechanisms) is that it can make people react inappropriately when dealing with information risk. External, exotic, unfamiliar threats are so often treated with more vigour than those generated close to home – even if the familiar threat has greater potential to cause harm.

I have already alluded to a specific survival mechanism in the preceding chapter (in the section 'Why do accidents happen?'). There are many of these, most of which have occasional unexpected effects.

Risk perception and familiarity changes over time. After the 11 September event in the US, air travellers became immediately tolerant of increased waiting times in airports. My experience of US internal air travel reminded me more of bus or rail travel in the UK, in that checks were minimal, and

---

**Survival Mechanisms**

We have a number of inbuilt mechanisms designed to help us survive. The best known of these is the 'flight or fight' reaction. This reaction diverts blood to the extremities and away from the internal organs (to fuel the muscles). Various hormones and other chemicals kick in to increase the pain threshold. The body starts to sweat, and digestion stops. Unfortunately for us, the threats that elicit this response these days (a row with the boss, traffic jams and so on) are not related to fighting or fleeing, so the reaction is wasted. As we don't fight or run away, it actually harms our bodies (high blood pressure, ulcers, heart trouble and so on) and does us no good at all. We can't ignore the reaction – it's inbuilt. Our innate fear and uncertainty about the unfamiliar is another such mechanism – and we have to recognize this as we try and communicate effectively in regard to risk and security.

---

boarding times short. The increased tolerance of inconvenience brought about by increased security checks after 11 September of US internal air travellers was understandable. Equally understandable was the slow decrease in this tolerance. One commentator described the situation as follows:

> *Suddenly that national guardsman starts to look more like a 22-year-old kid with 45 minutes of training with an M-16.*

The feeling of security provided by a heavily armed presence decreases inexorably. Europeans did not notice the increased security in international airports because most are used to it as a matter of course.

It's important to realize that actively *decreasing* security or threat levels after a raised period is often very important, especially if nothing has happened. To do so can make the security function look as if it's listening and thinking. A perpetually raised security level brings disrepute.

An example of such disrepute was the use of e-mail content checking. Around the end of the 1990s there was a surge of concern regarding the potential impact on companies of corporate e-mails containing profane language, and obscene content being made public. This concern was driven by fear of litigation and damage to 'the corporate brand'. The initial reaction was to install software that would check e-mail content, and block those messages that were deemed potentially damaging. These early systems were crude, and often deleted messages rather than storing them for further analysis. Security managers often deemed words like 'sex' amongst many others should be blocked. I live in the English county of Sussex. I was perturbed how many of my messages (both inbound and outbound) were being blocked. It was only when the content checking tool was analysed that this rather silly situation was dealt with.

Another example of familiarity impacting on how security is managed is the way in which security managers perceive local levels of threat and risk. Many years ago I worked for about 18 months in the Housing Department of Aberdeen City Council. My job involved the collection of rent arrears, which sometimes culminated in the eviction of tenants. One of the senior managers asked me one day what percentage of tenants I thought were in arrears with their rent. I suggested about 15 per cent. The actual figure was 2 per cent (amongst the best in the UK). My close involvement with the matter had caused me to internally exaggerate the numbers. For the same reason, information security managers see hackers on every corner. This phenomenon relates to the need to decrease controls once a threat has passed or when the initial reaction to a threat is seen as being excessive.

Information security professionals often overlook the manner in which their own perceptions impact on risk. Anne Adams and Angela Sasse of University College London have argued[2] that accidental compromise of password systems by users are the result of a degree of ignorance *and the manner in which controls have been implemented,* which are the result of the threat and risk perceptions of information security managers.

Adams and Sasse developed a questionnaire-based survey to determine user information regarding behaviour and perceptions regarding passwords and their use. The results provide a number of insights, including:

- Having to remember many different passwords for different systems is difficult and leads to poor password selection. The security professional concept of best practice, familiar to information security managers, is often impractical. Users perceive their choice of passwords as being driven by the process that is forced upon them. One of the results of this is that many users write their passwords down.

- Many users thought that using a piece of personal information (spouse's name, car registration and so on) to be *good* practice

2    Adams A and Sasse M A, 'Users are not the enemy', *Communications of the ACM*, 42/12 (1999).

– an idea at odds with that accepted by most information security professionals. When processes are introduced to prevent password reuse and the use of supposedly 'weak' passwords, this can lead to poorer security, as more users write their passwords down.

There is another impact on security that occurs during this process that is hard to quantify, and has significant potential for harm. The credibility of and regard for security decreases as users realize they have to circumvent supposedly rational controls in order to get on with their work.

Further results from this study are enlightening. Prime amongst these are that users are not sufficiently informed regarding information security issues, in that they have to 'construct their own model of possible *security threats* and the *importance of security* and these are often wildly inaccurate'. Users determined that certain systems and types of information were important (such as human resources and staff information), but ignored other assets which could be the root of significant harm should they be compromised.

The result of this is that users compromise systems either because they don't know they are important, or because they perceive the system to be unimportant. Adams and Sasse hold the concept of 'need to know' in a degree of contempt, in that they feel it can in many circumstances (perhaps outside government and the military) actually reduce security. The perceptions held by security professionals are at the root of these problems, and this is based on familiarity with what is thought 'best practice'.

## PSYCHOLOGY OF RISK OR 'WHY DO PEOPLE DO STUPID THINGS?'

How often have you asked yourself 'Why on earth did I do that?' Why do train drivers run red lights? Why do airline pilots sometimes turn left when clearly told to turn right?

There are reasons behind seemingly inexplicable behaviour, and most of these are firmly based in social psychology.

### DEFENCE MECHANISMS

The human psyche is extremely good at setting up defences against painful events, a phenomenon that some refer to as 'seeking peace of mind' – a state that many people understandably find pleasant. It can manifest in small ways, such as hiding scary bills behind the mantelpiece clock, to huge events, such as distancing oneself from multiple deaths, as was the case with many military leaders during the First World War.

Norman Dixon, in his seminal work *On the Psychology of Military Incompetence*[3], provides a very clear sketch as to how these defences can build to such an extent that senior military men can hide behind their defences (in the physical world, many miles behind their defences!) and produce the most crass, insensible and seemingly idiotic decisions as regards the prosecution of successful warfare. Dixon, in another related work *Our Own Worst Enemy*[4], suggests that two aspects of human psychology come into play to provide this peace of mind. These are 'selective attention' and the 'affective signalling system' (ASS). Selective attention is a means by which people can search for very specific things, such as water, food and potential mates. It can apparently be seen in the way men do supermarket shopping – they are much more focused than women, perhaps because their sense of selective attention is more developed. They go in, get what they want, ignore everything else, and get out.

Affective signalling is the basis of the term 'affective disorder'. Affective disorders are behavioural patterns that emerge as a result of this system failing and producing unwanted effects. The ASS is used to provide motivation to meet a need (that is, it makes you feel hungry when you need food), and then provide another signal to stop the behaviour (it makes further food intake unpleasant once you've eaten enough). The system is complex, and its breakdown can cause unexpected and unwanted events, ranging from overeating to murder. One of the results of such a breakdown is the development of defence mechanisms such as repression, denial, rationalization, isolation and projection.

For information security practitioners, the impact of such defences is all too common. For example, many people deny (to themselves) the possibility of catastrophic failure, rationalizing by saying 'it's never happened here before', despite the fact that they are presented with considerable empirical evidence that it's going to happen at some point. 'Shooting the messenger' is another manifestation of these defences; the temptation is to project feelings of anger onto a thing or person that is not directly involved. The results of such behaviour can become part of an unhealthy organization (see the section 'Corporate health' in Chapter 2), and can result in a reduction in security as motivation for reporting events reduces.

---

3    Dixon Norman F, *On thePsychology of Military Incompetence,* Jonathon Cape (1979).
4    Dixon Norman F, *Our Own Worst Enemy*, Jonathon Cape (1987).

Seeking peace of mind has a considerable effect on the decision-making process. When faced with a number of possible potential outcomes, people will often decide to accept the one that is least threatening, even when evidence for other less palatable options is more compelling. This factor can affect risk perception and decision making – even memory. Many of these factors combine to massively reduce competence, and make the job of applying appropriate controls, and of convincing people to apply appropriate controls, extremely difficult.

## MEMORY

Selective memory (often a result of defence mechanisms) creates problems for us in two areas: the first relates to peace of mind, the other to 'absent mindedness'. The reason why people are forgetful (and seemingly stupid) is often because they have only a limited capacity for information. It is well understood that many people have problems assimilating information whilst trying to perform a complex task. This is the main reason why using a mobile phone when driving is so dangerous (even when using a hands-free set).

One of the significant influences that can affect memory is stress. When people are stressed, they become extremely focused on a particular job in hand – an admirable trait when confronted with an immediate threat to life or limb. It can become a problem when dealing with complex situations. This has been amply illustrated by examples of pilots crashing planes despite advanced warning devices and assisting electronics. Pilots can become focused on a single issue and *exclude* signals from other sources. Our consciousness is limited by this trait, and can make rational people do seemingly irrational things. One of the tasks of an awareness programme is to try and interrupt this process and encourage people to stop, maybe only momentarily, and ask themselves whether the situation has a security element to it.

## GROUPTHINK

People in groups make decisions in different ways to individuals. Part of this group dynamic is responsible for many mistakes – be they military, medical, technical or commercial. This is not to say that all group decisions cause mistakes – there is plentiful evidence that coherent, cohesive groups can make sound, rounded decisions that an individual could not.

Irving Janis, a social psychologist based at Yale, has defined groupthink as:

> ...*a mode of thinking that people engage in when they are deeply involved in a cohesive in-group, when the members' strivings for unanimity override their motivation to realistically appraise alternative courses of action.*[5]

It seems that the syndrome causes greater emphasis to be placed on group harmony and cohesiveness than the critical assessment of the subject in hand. I'm sure I have felt the personal impact of groupthink many times. I'm convinced it's related to the 'Noddy Effect' (see overleaf). Try to say 'no' during a meeting when everyone else is being positive. If groupthink is kicking in, you will find this very hard to do – it's human nature. Going against the grain in a warm, cohesive peer group is tough.

Groupthink has lead to numerous disasters: the Challenger Space Shuttle explosion being one[6]; the invasion of Iraq in 2003 could be another.

Janis suggested that there are eight basic symptoms of groupthink, these being:

- illusion of invulnerability
- belief in inherent morality of the group
- collective rationalization
- out-group stereotypes
- self-censorship
- illusion of unanimity
- direct pressure on dissenters
- self-appointed mindguards.

Methods to help avoid groupthink include:

- placing responsibility for distinct decisions onto individuals;
- selecting, in advance, a person who will perform the role of devil's advocate. This reduces the potential social discomfort of disagreeing, and ensures flaws are actually aired;

---

5    Janis Irving, *Victims of Groupthink,* Houghton Mifflin (1972).
6    Griffin Em, *A First Look at Communication Theory,* Chapter 18, McGraw-Hill (1997).

- anonymous channels for comments (attitude surveys or suggestion boxes for example).

---

**The Noddy Effect**

This effect occurs during meetings when groupthink is beginning to take hold. Once one person begins to act in an affirmative manner (and in doing so, many people subconsciously begin to nod their heads), the rest begin to join in. The human ability to detect and react to the tiniest of subliminal signals is amazing. Try it yourself. Nod gently during meetings when a positive decision is being requested by one of the meeting attendees. People will follow your lead, and very gently nod back at you, especially if you catch their eye. The effect spreads round the meeting, and opposing the decision request become increasingly difficult. If you are in a meeting that is trying to make risk-based decisions (such as agreeing on an awareness initiative), make sure that groupthink does not kick in. Oppose the Noddy effect as early as you can.

---

## USER MINDSETS

Having established that standards, best practice and professional opinion suggest awareness is essential; we are faced with a particular problem. We do not understand the mindset of users very well – often because we tend to be parochial. To illustrate how security is perceived, Sasse, Brostoff and Weirich[7] identified seven issues that lead to unwanted behaviour relating to password use. These are:

### Identity issues

People who exhibit good password behaviour are often described as 'paranoid', 'pedantic' or 'the kind of person who doesn't trust anybody' – even by themselves. Some participants are proud of the fact that they do not understand security ('I'm not a nerd'), or do not comply with regulations ('I don't just follow orders').

---

7    Sasse M A, Brostoff S and Weirich D, 'Transforming the "weakest link" – a human/computer interaction approach to usable and effective security', *BT Technology Journal,* 19/3 (2001).

## Social issues

Sharing your password is considered by many users to be a sign of trust in their colleagues – you share your password with people you trust, and somebody refusing to share their password with you is effectively telling you that they do not trust you. The same goes for other password-related behaviour, such as locking your screen when you leave your computer for a few minutes – you are telling your colleagues next to you that you do not trust them.

## Nobody will target me

Most users think the data stored on their system is not important enough to become the target of a hacker or industrial spy. Hackers, for example, are assumed to target rich and famous people or institutions. Some users accept that hackers might target somebody like them just to get into the overall system and try to get further from there, but clearly do not regard this as very likely, purely because of the number of users that could be targeted this way.

## They couldn't do much damage anyway

Most users do not think that somebody getting into their account could cause any serious harm to them or their organization.

## Informal work procedures

Current password mechanisms and regulations often clash with formal or informal work procedures (for example, if you are ill and cannot come into work, somebody in your group should be able to access your account and take care of your business).

## Accountability

Most users are aware that their behaviour does not fully comply with security regulations. However, they do not expect to be made accountable because they regard the regulations as unrealistic and their behaviour as common practice. In addition, they know that there is always a chance that a hacker will break into their system, however well they behave. They can always claim that it was not their misbehaviour that led to the break-in.

Some users do realize that they might be held accountable for past behaviour (for example, writing down their password) if somebody gets into their system now.

### Double-binds

If a computer system has strong security mechanisms, it is more likely to come under attack from hackers who want to prove themselves, and who will in the end find a way to get in. If it has weak security, inexperienced hackers, who try to break into many systems without targeting one specifically, might get in.

Similarly, if you follow rules (for example, lock your screen), people will think you have valuable data on your computer, and are more likely to try to break in. But if you do not follow regulations, it is easier for somebody to break in.

## SCHEMAS

One important characteristic of information security practice is that it can arouse emotions – sometimes significant emotions. Information security practitioners can be accused of being obstructive and unnecessarily authoritarian. This can lead to people circumventing controls – whilst believing that they are doing the right thing.

The aroused emotion (normally anger) is the result of a conflict between the schema used by security people and those who have a different view of the world. A schema is just that, a view of the world. It provides a framework within which we can make rapid decisions. A schema helps us concentrate on what we believe to be important, and to ignore things that we deem unimportant, thereby helping us make these rapid decisions.

Unfortunately, as stated above, the schemas used by security people often conflict with those used by others. As an example, in most work environments, one of the main aspects of the work schema is the ethic of teamwork. This involves *inter alia* sharing, civility and respect. One of the main tenets of physical security in office buildings is that 'you must challenge anyone who is not wearing an appropriate ID badge'. I find this personally extremely difficult – probably because I like to be nice to others. The result is a decided clash between the rules and the normal schema.

I remember a specific instance of a company where the computer operators controlled the access to the head office building out of hours. They had a simple intercom system between the main door and the operations centre, and would walk up from the operations centre to open the main door to admit those they deemed had the right to access. The operators would normally admit people they knew (normally cleaners, colleagues and other service staff). There was an ID badge scheme, and when they failed to recognize a person, they would ask to see it. On one occasion, a member of the board (who, like many board members, was totally anonymous to the staff) demanded access outside normal hours. The reason he needed access was to recover a small non-work item from his desk. The operator on duty did not know who he was – and the board member had no ID card (he actually felt such things 'were not for him'). The operator refused him access. The board member tried to bully his way in, and the following day, tried to have the operator sacked. I'm glad to say he failed – indeed, he was removed from his post about a month afterwards. I suggest that the board member's schema was very different from the operator's.

One important characteristic of a schema involves people who are presented with information that contradicts their own schema, especially if it reaches them amongst a stream of information that otherwise reinforces their schema. In this circumstance they will normally discard that information.[8] This selective retention and rejection have a number of effects, not least a reduction in the ability to learn. I suspect it can also explain how many people make errors (see section Psychology of risk or 'Why do people do stupid things?' in Chapter 1). This characteristic of schemas has to be borne in mind as you try and change behaviour. Anyone can assimilate new information if they are given time to digest it (and thereby change their world view), and provided there is a limit to the amount of new information presented. *This suggests that changing people's minds involves a steady, strategic approach rather than a tactical big bang of change.*

Changing schemas require their components to be challenged actively. The best way to do this is to provide realistic examples that the target audiences can truly relate to that are counter to each element of the schema. The common habit of information sharing most people have in offices can be countered by emphasizing the *personal* protection you have if you keep your password to yourself. People do not perceive risk in a linear manner, and that the use of examples, stories and illustrations is much more effective than the delivery of tabulated statistics. We can use this basic human characteristic to our advantage – if the media distort the truth and help establish unhelpful schemas through broad statements, sweeping generalities and weighted terminology, then we can respond in kind.

---

8    Lippa R A, *Introduction to Social Psychology (1ˢᵗ ed.)*, Belmont (1990).

## THE BYSTANDER EFFECT

The bystander effect is a term that defines the tendency for a group of people to be less likely than a single individual to help a person in trouble. A bystander often experiences embarrassment, not knowing how to help, and very often feels a lack of responsibility. The incident that sparked the academic work that spawned the term was the murder in 1964 in New York of a woman called Kitty Genovese. She was very publicly stabbed to death while people watched and did nothing to help her.

Social psychologists Latane and Darnley[9] researched the phenomenon and discovered the reasons why this happens. They demonstrated that helping behaviour follows a model that involves five stages:

- noticing the problem;

- deciding if it is an emergency;

- taking responsibility;

- deciding what to do;

- taking action to help.

The work suggests that when a person is in trouble they are better off to be around one or two people than in a crowd. As the group size increases a person's sense of responsibility decreases because they feel that someone else will do something.

If there are many people in the vicinity a person's sense of responsibility diminishes.

The resulting conclusions we can make from this phenomenon are many. The main one relates to the reporting of incidents. If we fail to make people feel responsible, they will not report an incident, if they feel they can get away with it – it becomes somebody else's problem. Douglas Adams (1980) described an imaginary field for hiding large objects from view in the second of the four books in his *Hitchhiker's Guide to the Galaxy* trilogy as follows:

---

9    Latane D and Darley J, *The unresponsive bystander: Why doesn't he help?*, Appleton-Century-Crofts (1968).

*The Somebody Else's Problem field is much simpler and more effective, and what's more can be run for over a hundred years on a single torch battery. This is because it relies on people's natural disposition not to see anything they don't want to, weren't expecting, or can't explain.*

The Restaurant at the End of the Universe

The phenomenon is used by muggers on the London Underground. The tactic is to start an argument with a person using personal names – suggesting to onlookers that the people involved know each other. This one factor greatly reduces the chances of other people intervening.

## SUMMARY

- Remember that people often come to conclusions on illogical grounds through illogical routes. The fact is, they often think that they have been logical. Do not be surprised – indeed, expect seemingly illogical decisions. The people involved aren't stupid. They are simply the victims of their own inbuilt legacy. Remember that you also have the same inbuilt flaws.

- Different people perceive things in different ways. What you consider risky, they may well consider incidental. What they think is good practice, you consider to be foolhardy.

- People do not calculate risk in any logical or linear manner. There are multiplicities of factors that affect their perception. If you fail to recognize this, your ability to communicate effectively will be reduced.

- Risk communication requires thought and understanding. Avoid jargon when talking to a non-specialist audience. Illustrate any examples you have in terms they can understand – verbal pictures can be extremely useful.

- Never try and deceive your audience – they will find out and your loss of credibility can have ongoing effects.

- Memory is fallible. People often forget things for a reason. This affects their decision-making process and their ability to react to changing circumstances.

- When you are confronted with negative groupthink, you should break the spell as soon as possible. Remember that you will meet opposition from the mindguards and other minions. Your main defence is factual. Stick to the facts, and keep highlighting your opponent's assumptions.

- Remember that incremental change, rather than a big-bang approach is more effective in generating permanent change. This is especially so if you involve those affected by the changes in the change process itself.

- Understand your target audience mindset, and use this as one of the foundations of your awareness work. To change behaviour, we have to understand why people operate in particular ways. If you can alter your audience *schema*, you stand a much better chance of changing their behaviour.

- We are aiming to help people attain a state of 'rational alertness'. You must present security as a rational state – never paranoid or nerdish. Never portray poor security practice in a positive light – it can be seen as cool to operate outside regulation. This is especially true when the regulatory framework is seen as irrational (too oppressive, overly constrictive or otherwise inappropriate). Appropriate control (that has been accepted by your targets) will succeed much more readily than oppression or diktat.

Never let people become bystanders. They have to feel they own the information security problem. You must engage them by helping them recognize that there is a problem, that they have a responsibility for dealing with the problem, and that they will be found out if they do nothing!

# CHAPTER 2

# *Security Culture*

There's an old saying: 'Whenever I hear the word culture, I reach for my gun.' Culture is an overused word, but it is an aspect of any organization that has a significant bearing on the way that it operates. Information security is in many ways a young subject, and other disciplines have made greater progress in the study of the effects of culture on business or industrial operations.

Nevertheless, since information security is primarily about the behaviour of employees, understanding and influencing the culture in which they operate is paramount.

## WHAT IS CULTURE?

An organizational culture can be defined as 'a shared system of norms (values) and beliefs', or 'an amalgamation of individual and group values, attitudes, perceptions and behavioural patterns'. It can also be said to be 'a complex pattern of beliefs, expectations, ideas, values, attitudes and behaviors in an organization that binds members together and influences what they think about themselves and what they do'.[1] Some analysts use the term 'dominant values' as a means of identifying elements of culture. For example, if a company is essentially service led, common terms such as 'customer first' tend to pop up as manifestations of such values. Examples of other manifestations of culture include working patterns (do people regularly perform unpaid overtime work?) and such things as dress codes.

What is notable about culture is that it has developed over a long time, and is transmitted through multiple carriers, including 'mythology' (often termed 'urban legends'), peers, mentors and so on. Formal management is not the sole carrier – indeed, it may have only a minor part to play in the entire process. Therefore, any attempt to impose a new culture (be it sales, safety or security) will meet with resistance.

Large organizations contain many formal rules, regulations, policies, standards and working practices. Most organizations work on the basis of informal rules and loosely based social alliances (often referred to as the

---

1    Hellreigle D, Slocum J and Woodman R, *Organizational Behavior* (1998).

'unwritten rules'). It is ironic that one of the most effective means by which staff can put pressure on management during a dispute is by 'working to rule'.

In the UK, the Ministry of Defence (MoD) has a fully established culture that demands that desks be cleared at the end of each working day, and that classified papers are locked into suitable cabinets or similar, depending on the sensitivity of the information involved. Given the nature of the information handled by the MoD, such a clear-desk regime is relatively easy to implement. In other cultures, a clear-desk policy remains one of the distant holy grails of information security management.

---

### Clear-desk Policy

Clear-desk policies are often seen by those that don't follow them as draconian. I find this unhelpful. Clearing your desk at the end of each day makes a lot of sense. As well as protecting sensitive information from theft and prying eyes, it can have side benefits as follows. Paper can withstand heat (provided it does not meet an open flame), and provided it is kept dry, has a long life. If you leave your work on your desktop each night, you expose yourself to the obvious risks of theft and disclosure. If there's a fire, it is more likely to burn. If it doesn't burn, it is more likely to be exposed to water damage (from sprinklers and fire hoses). If windows are blown out, the papers are more likely to be disrupted (even lost) due to draughts and the wind. As the work on your desk is normally 'work in progress', it is unlikely to have a backup.

Security people make the mistake of demanding that you lock your work away each night, or ask that you extract the sensitive papers for the same treatment. I have heard users say that their lock is broken or they don't have room for a lockable cabinet. Forget complex locking and extraction policies – just ask people to put their stuff away in a drawer each night. This reduces the risk of damage or loss through theft, fire, water and wind (earthquakes even)! You are much more likely to get people to conform to such a simple request – especially when you tell them why you're asking them.

## CORPORATE HEALTH

Closely linked to the concept of culture is that of corporate 'health'. This does not confine itself to fiscal health – rather to an idea of balanced risk. An unhealthy organization is likely to be an insecure organization. Over-control can be as devastating as a lack of control. I once had to work with a head auditor who insisted on the use of a control termed 'enter and check'.

The original enter and check process involved a senior programmer checking previously entered program codes by replicating what a junior programmer had just done. Errors were quickly spotted. In its context, this control is rational and appropriate. It is totally inappropriate when used to check the quality of text-based information being entered into a database. In this example the source of the data was a hand-written form. The entry screens were essentially free-text (perhaps with some numeric fields). This led to inevitable differences between the data input by the enterer and that by the checker. The potential for transposition of characters, spelling mistakes and character misinterpretation (handwriting is sometimes extremely hard to interpret) is considerable.

The control was used during a time of big increases in business volume, and the staff had ever-growing piles of work. The inevitable happened. In order to keep up with the level of demand, employees began to cheat. They hid piles of work, they took sick leave and then began to share passwords. This problem was compounded by the introduction of an additional control, a specialist piece of software that checked the validity of the postcode or zip code. People do not always put the correct code on their forms. Staff discovered that there was a particular postcode that worked in all circumstances (it was a test code originally used by the developers). The result was a serious decrease in the integrity of the database, which came to a head when the marketing department attempted to create a mailing list for new customers using the postcode as the key field. The resulting mess (which included demotions, sackings and considerable expense) was largely caused by over-control – in itself a sure sign of corporate ill health. It is essential that any attempts to imbue a security culture do not impact on corporate health.

What is a healthy organization? The main characteristic is probably what is known as an 'affiliative attitude'. This concept has been described in great detail by the late psychiatrist Robin Skynner and the comedian John Cleese in their book *Life and How to Survive It*. It includes the following characteristics:

- trust

- openness

- tolerance for independence

- being allowed to make mistakes.

Their ethos is summed up in the following brief extract:

> **John** *They must have heard the old English proverb, 'He who does not make mistakes is unlikely to make anything.'*

> **Robin** *Very good. In fact, in the healthiest companies the taboo is not on mistakes. It's on concealing them!*

Skynner and Cleese make great play on the effect unhealthy practices have on the effectiveness (aka profitability) of organizations. I suggest that they will have a similar, significant effect on security. A blame culture can stifle information flow, and create circumstances that encourage poor security practice.

One of the four (possibly five) main tenets of information security is decent management information.[2] This information is the basis of step one of the stepped approach set out in Chapter 4 – which is founded on a principle called 'managing by fact'. Without information, you are blind. If you don't know what risks you face, you have no idea where to invest your time and budget. Without decent management information, you cannot operate effectively.

In an unhealthy organization, one of the prime traits you will see is poor information flow. This is often because people are too scared to report events simply because they know that there is a tendency to shoot the messenger. Others will seek to distort facts (and omit facts) simply because they do not want to be seen to have made a mistake. The result is poor management information, which results in distorted risk assessment, which leads to poor investment decisions, and in turn to ineffective security.

If you are operating in an unhealthy organization, you have a number of choices. You can:

---

2    The four (possibly five) are:
- Management information (including event logging and monitoring)
- Education, training and awareness
- Policy and governance
- Access control management
- Joiners, leavers and transferees (this could be part of access control management)

- leave – an option I have taken more than once – there's no point in beating your head against a brick wall;

- recognize the effect this situation brings, and manage your work accordingly;

- try and change the culture from within.

This latter option is probably the most honest and the most difficult. It sums up one of the main issues discussed in this book – change is difficult, and changing people is the hardest of all.

What then do you do in an unhealthy organization? I suggest the following:

- Be honest and straightforward in all your dealings. Don't play the game – you will get sucked in if you do.

- Remember that many people's motivation has nothing whatsoever to do with the stated aims of the organization – but are everything to do with their own aims, objectives and possibly even survival.

One of the main characteristics of any healthy entity (person, corporation, family and so on) is that of balance. When trying to develop metrics for measuring the relative success of different departments in large organizations, the concept of the balanced score card has been developed. The key word here again is 'balanced'. You can seek to determine how well a department has performed in terms of:

- money

- people

- processes.

These can also be expressed as below, when different aspects of an organization establishes (and meets) particular needs:

- finance – establishes financial needs

- customer – establishes customer needs

- internal processes – establishes key processes

- learning and growth – establishes staff needs.

The strongest aspect of corporate health is balance. A security positive environment is not necessarily a disciplined dictatorship wherein everyone does what they are told. I suggest the following traits as beneficial and desirable:

- People report security incidents, even if they happen in their own backyard.

- People are aware of security issues.

- People want to enhance the security of the organization.

- Nobody shoots the messenger.

- Communication exists up, down, left and right.

Once this culture is established you have the option of managing with information, rather than in the dark. Without this option, your job is almost impossible.

## THEORY X – THEORY Y

Allied to health are some further concepts that need to be explored when considering the nature and impact of corporate cultures. The best known of these is Theory X – Theory Y.

Theory X and Theory Y were described by Douglas McGregor[3] (an American social psychologist) to illustrate two belief systems. McGregor proposed his theory in his 1960 book *The Human Side of Enterprise*. Theory X suggested that people didn't want to work, and had to be cajoled, bullied and forced into action. Theory Y contrasted this view with one that suggested that people are keen, co-operative and self-starting. McGregor's work has remained valid for years, and his principles are used constantly in other studies on organizational management and development.

McGregor suggested that managers who tend towards Theory X tend to perform less well, and do not get the best results from their staff. Theory X is an authoritarian management style.

Theory Y can be described as participatory, and avoids threats, and suggests most people actually thrive on responsibility, are ambitious and do not seek personal security as the main aim of their work.

---

3    McGregor D, *The Human Side of Enterprise* (1960).

Theory Y suggests that work is as natural as anything else, and that people love to use their imagination and creative abilities. Public supporters of Theory Y include Robert Townsend (former chief of Avis and author of the classic business tome *Up the Organization*[4]) and Waterman & Peters, authors of *In Search of Excellence*[5] amongst many other books.

Peters has suggested that you ask your staff to write down the things they do in their spare time. He cites a number of examples of skill and ability that may not be obvious. Some people played classical music to an expert degree. Others ran theatre companies on demanding shoestring budgets. These people did not apply themselves at work with the same diligence. Peters was keen to ask why? In a Theory X environment, the question is probably never asked, and the potential people-based benefits never realized.

If you are trying to operate in a Theory X world, you need to recognize the main characteristics of the Theory X manager. Symptoms include:

- arrogant, detached and distant;

- delegates risk to juniors, but never the rewards;

- has a short fuse that manifests through shouting and aggression;

- has no concern for staff welfare, and never gives out praise or offers thanks;

- has no empathy with staff, and thinks morale is irrelevant;

- has no interest in participatory and team-oriented work styles;

- is a cheapskate, both in terms of salaries and the awarding of expenses;

- issues ultimatums (often using deadlines);

- manages through impractical deadlines and deliverables, often to no good purpose;

- never makes a request, but will issue a demand;

- obsessive dedication to results and deadlines, even when they are seen over time to be not in the best interest of the organization;

---

4    Townsend R, *Up the Organization: How to Stop the Corporation from Stifling People and Strangling Profits*, Knopf: New York (1970).
5    Peters T and Waterman R, *In Search of Excellence*, Harper Row: New York (1982).

- operates a blame culture, often looking for the guilty party (failing to learn from mistakes in the process);

- operates in broadcast mode most of the time – is rarely in receive mode;

- operates via orders, instructions and threats;

- poor at investing in future success;

- snobbish and overly proud – sometimes elitist;

- unable to tolerate outsiders and people who disagree;

- retains the ownership of the benefits of work (such as bonuses) but will shed accountability onto junior staff;

- retaliates against people when criticized, and will fail to accept suggestions.

Does this sound like anyone you know?

## CONFORMITY V COMPLIANCE

Closely related to the Theory X/Y concepts above is the contrast between the concepts of conformity and compliance. These are terms used by social psychologists to describe two different ways in which people are motivated.

Conformity tends to be driven by forces internal to a person, such as wanting to be part of a group. The ultimate element of conformity is that the behaviours it engenders are almost subconscious.

Compliance tends to be externally imposed, normally in conjunction with a scheme of reward and/or punishment. People *comply* because they feel they have to, or believe that the cost (financial, emotional, social and so on) of not complying is too high.

The problem with compliance is that in order for it to work, it needs to be policed. Policing (also known to some as auditing) is expensive. Making people comply requires constant reinforcement, and this also costs.

Although the process of attaining conformity can be lengthy and costly, in the long term (that is strategically) it is nearly always cheaper and more effective. The following quote illustrates this well:

*When enforcing security policies, too many organizations focus entirely on punishing those who break the rules. However, everything we know about modifying behaviour teaches us to use reward rather than punishment. A security officer in a large corporation experimented with reward and punishment in implementing security policies. Employees were supposed to log off their terminals when leaving the office, but compliance rates were only around 40 per cent. In one department, the security officer used the usual techniques: putting up nasty notes on terminals that were not logged off, reporting violators to their bosses, and changing the passwords on delinquent accounts. In a different department, she simply identified those users who had indeed logged off their terminals and left a Hershey's Chocolate Kiss on the keyboard. After one month, compliance rates in the department subject to punishment had climbed to around 50 per cent. Compliance in the department getting chocolates had reached 80 per cent.[6]*

## APPETITE FOR RISK

Some organizations thrive on taking risks – investment banks for example. They could never be described as 'risk-averse'. Risk management is normally reflected in all their processes – they hold little store in precisely defined security procedures (this is due in part to the lack of patience of many of their front-desk employees).

Risk appetite varies in other ways. People will often make positive risk decisions based on very long odds *if* there is the prospect of extremely high payoffs (how else would the numerous national and state lotteries run across the world remain in business?)

Most of us are prepared to gamble on long odds for the chance of a huge gain – the same is true of insurance. We will pay (normally and statistically at a loss) premiums to protect us against low-probability high-impact losses (such as early death and house fires). Many of the problems we associate with obtaining investment in information security are based on a lack of understanding of the risks being run. There are so many uncertainties operating that many senior managers (normally budget holders) go into denial, hiding behind the 'it's never happened here' syndrome.

---

6    Kabay M (ed), 'Using Social Psychology to Implement Security Policies', *Computer Security Handbook,* John Wiley & Sons (2002).

## NATIONAL CULTURE

I was working in a major EU institution that was composed of all nationalities from across the EU. My client contact was Austrian, who spoke perfect French and English as well as his native German. He introduced me to the concept of Anglo-Saxon attitudes, suggesting I was imbued with them. The Anglo-Saxon bloc is considered to be the UK, North America and Australasia. There are undoubtedly numerous other pockets lurking around the world – the Netherlands is sometimes included.

His observations on his colleagues were fascinating; the 'southerns' (Italian, Portuguese, Greek and so on) went to eat at different times from the 'northerns' (Germans, Swedes, Danes and so on). Further differences were observed in the manner meetings were held, the way power and influence were wielded, and the manner and means of communication with staff and colleagues.

Prejudice has its roots in fear and ignorance, and perceived differences between national, religious and racial groups can be exploited. Not in this man's case – his observations were made as empirically as was possible, and are backed up by research, notably by Hofstede.

Hofstede[7] performed research into the way in which different national groups behaved within IBM. This research took place over many years. He suggested that there are four dimensions that describe the differences between various cultures. These are:

- *Power distance* – power distance is the dimension that is measured by the difference between bosses and subordinates in terms of corporate power. Large power distances indicate a more dictatorial regime than one with a smaller distance.

- *Uncertainty avoidance* – high uncertainty avoidance is associated with traditionalism, conservatism and dogma. It even has a hint of superstition to it.

- *Individualism* – individualism (as opposed to collectivism) is high in the Anglo-Saxon bloc, and lower in other nations, notably in parts of South America and South East Asia.

- *Masculinity* – masculinity relates to power, ambition and quantity. The opposite, femininity, relates to interpersonal relations and service-oriented themes.

---

7    Hofstede G, *Culture's Consequences* (1980).

Further research by Mant[8] put Hofstede's research into charts, and depicted graphically the differences between eight nations. The biggest contrasts were between the Scandinavians and the Japanese. The differences are so great that Mant postulates that Japanese techniques of management would fail utterly in the individualistic, low power distance, low uncertainty avoidance, feminine Nordic countries. Anglo-Saxons are individualistic, low power distance, low uncertainty avoidance and masculine.

We have established that national characteristics do therefore have an impact on corporate culture. We therefore have to consider how these differences impact on information security education and awareness. This manifests most obviously in the audiences we have to consider.

What works for a Swede will not necessarily work for an Italian. I recall my own personal reaction to some Danish security education initiatives. I found myself reacting against some of it for being 'too nice'. I felt it needed a bit more assertion. My Danish colleagues felt I was being very formal and harsh – 'too Anglo-Saxon' suggested one. Later, I was fascinated to see an English colleague struggle to convince a Spanish audience of the need for discipline in the systems development process – he failed to recognize his own perceived rigidity – and found himself confused by his audience's seeming slackness. The solution is to recognize and empathize with your audience's perception of you, their work in general and security in particular.

## CULTURAL EXAMPLES

There is always a danger when describing examples garnered through experience that you begin to pander to stereotypes and personal prejudices. I have developed a series of heuristics (rules of thumb) that help me rapidly ascertain the types of organization and characters that I am dealing with, especially when working for the first time in a new industry or sector. These cultural examples are based on much of the thinking set out above, but are essentially a distillation of my own experience, observations and research. This personal approach works for me; I appreciate that they are unlikely to be universally applicable.

It is also important to note that operating in this generic manner will always unearth exceptions. In the sections below, I contrast some of the perceived characteristics of retail bank culture with investment banks. The two worlds

---

8    Mant A, *Leaders We Deserve* (1983).

are not mutually exclusive: there are plenty of retail bankers who are forceful, results driven and prone to risk taking; there are investment bankers who are process driven, methodical and structured in their thinking. I don't think this adversely impacts my examples, but do bear in mind their generic nature.

Please note that the examples reflect my own background in financial services.

## INVESTMENT BANK

An investment bank is, for the most part, focused on a single aim in life – making money – and lots of it. In their view, anything that distracts them from making money is a waste of time. If you suggest a change in procedure, or some additional task that reduces income or raises costs, you will get extremely short shrift. The language used is often acquisitive, aggressive and masculine. Dealing with these guys from an information security perspective can often be extremely difficult. There is a potential solution, the basis of which is found, bizarrely, in revolutionary communism.

---

### Ho Chi Minh

One of the most effective and underrated military leaders of all time was Ho Chi Minh, leader of the North Vietnamese initially against the French, and latterly, the USA. Perhaps his place in history is poorly documented because he did not conquer and subdue other lands, as did Alexander, Caesar and Bonaparte. He only fought in Vietnam (with a few excursions into Cambodia and Laos). His philosophy was based on leading from behind. He didn't have staff cars, aides-de-camp or welcoming bands. His only aim was victory. He ate the same food as his men, and gave them credit for everything. The result was the defeat of the USA. He won because his troops did it for themselves. You can achieve anything provided you are prepared to forego the credit. This is what Ho Chi Minh did. To make an investment banker do what you want, make him think it's his idea, and be prepared to forego credit.[9]

---

9 See Robert Townsend's *Up the Organization* (1970) for more on Ho Chi Minh.

This Ho Chi Minh technique works in many circumstances, not just for the driven culture of investment banking. Also note that this technique can be used in any situation where you have to negotiate strong egos and a strong professional focus. I've seen it work with groups of barristers, senior civil servants and management consultancies.

## RETAIL BANK

Retail banks live on instructions. I have seen the desk instructions for a normal bank clerk. They are written on A4 paper in volumes that stretch across a 2-metre shelf. They contain everything from how to assist people open a current account to how to deal with an unexpected influx of Krugerrands. There are instructions on money-laundering protection processes, the destruction of chequebooks and what to do in an armed bank raid.

They are, in many ways, the opposite of investment bankers. To be effective, you have to understand the appetite for instruction that exists at the commercial front line, appreciate the command and control nature of the business. One UK bank even refers to its retail operations department as 'manufacturing'.

To deal with retail banks in regard to awareness, you have to assimilate yourself into this structure, and become part of command and control. I suggest that you don't use this route as a single means of operating, and that the piggybacking onto internal communications is something that can be done in many circumstances. The descriptor 'retail bank' is not confined to the financial world – I find I can use it in many heavily documented process-oriented organizations, which include many government departments.

## EXCLUSIVE BANKS

I have to include exclusive banks because they are an unusual type, and sometimes require customized handling. I recall trying to foster agreement on a series of policies between a number of separate companies in a single financial group. They included an exclusive bank, an investment bank and all shades between the two. Whilst the investment bankers tried to minimize anything I offered, the exclusive bank asked very specifically to be told what to do – in some detail. They were even more process driven than the retail bank. They were, in information security terms, extremely easy to work with. They were also totally client centric, and very keen to do the right thing. The exclusive bank culture was one of client protection – sometimes to their commercial disadvantage.

If you pay attention to their client-centred focus, and create policies, instructions and guidance that mirror this ethic, you will have a good chance of making a difference to their security behaviours. Anything that strays outside this will be less effective. As an example, promoting certification to BS 7799 Part 2[10] as an aid to marketing will have less impact than demonstrating how certification can be used to provide assurance to the bank's high net-worth customer base that their money and personal information is being cared for appropriately.

## HIGH-TECH R&D

There's nothing like a collection of boffins (highly technically specialized research and development staff) for the creation of bespoke systems. They like them this way, normally for reasons that are operationally questionable, but these reasons are strongly felt, and their opinions strongly held.

I have seen non-standard e-mail and messaging systems implemented, preventing the effective deployment of anti-virus solutions and content-checking software. The reason often given for using this customized e-mail set up was that 'it is very elegant, in processor utilization terms'. Many boffins find beauty and elegance in the throughput of processor devices. This may have value but can be extremely detrimental to the security of the concern. This can be a bit worrying if the organization is dealing with sensitive material and information, such as technology defence contracts.

Another characteristic of these boffin-fuelled enterprises is the rather annoying fact that no matter how much you know about a technical issue (e-mail, viruses, cryptography and so on), there was always one of them who knew far, far more than you or any of your colleagues. This in-depth knowledge did not often extend to the practical implementation of these technologies, but it was often used as a barrier to progress.

The result of this culture is often a variegated technical landscape of bespoke implementations, with non-standard platforms (using every brand of Unix and Linux ever invented) running on exotic hardware (the arty end of the boffin field loves Apple Macs).

Boffins are not always confined to scientific research. The type appears in broadcasting (television broadcasters have hundreds of various custom developments running at capacity across multiple platforms).

---

10    BS 7799 Part 2: *Specification for information security management systems.*

They can be dealt with using the Ho Chi Minh approach (you have got to convince them it's their idea). You also have to realize that they are driven by non-profit factors, such as curiosity or the production of quality television programmes.

The strength of the boffin is that he or she is very intelligent, and if you present your case in a well-researched, factual manner, you can, if the case has merit, change their minds. Involving them in any risk-analysis process can make deep inroads into their prejudices. They can, with their deep skills and knowledge, add great value to the process, especially in the area of technical risk.

## LIFE INSURANCE

The City of Edinburgh has some of the most concentrated financial power in the world, much of it tied up in large life insurance concerns. This power is hidden quietly behind elegant architectural facades, and is exercised with discretion and caution. These giant life assurance companies own significant percentages of the UK stock market, and have investments spread across the world.[11]

Dealing with companies of this type requires a series of insights. First and foremost, the decision makers in these companies are often actuaries, and contrast sharply with such specimens as the dotcoms (see below). They are cautious, depend on fairly rigid financial business models, and have a time frame that extends into decades. Their investment profiles look to long-term growth rather than quick returns. Their primary concern is less that of confidentiality (although this is a factor), and rather more that of integrity. If their investment systems lose integrity, year one errors will become compounded across many years. The complexity of re-evaluating investment worth, especially when the integrity of the system is questionable, could impact enormously on the public profile of the organization. These companies live and die on their public profile, and damage to it can destroy an investment house.

These characteristics require you to recognize the importance of professional and informational integrity to these organizations. The tools and techniques that can be effective in broader financial organizations can fail easily in the life insurance business.

---

11  It has been reckoned that the Edinburgh financial services economy is about the same (in value terms) as that of the whole of Iran. One company was at one point thought to be as rich as the entire city of Vienna.

## DOTCOM

A dotcom culture is essentially that which develops during high-tech start-ups. The staff work extremely hard for long hours, and are often skilled, driven young people – often inexperienced. This heady mixture is ideal for this type of development, which requires drive, energy, creativity and resilience. What is often lacking is any regard for structure and process – which in many ways are the foundation of good security.

There seems to be a hiatus that is met around two years after actual start-up. Much depends on goodwill and best efforts up to this point. At two years, the painful realization that the organization has to grow up shocks some staff, and can lead to counterproductive internal bickering. This is as much the result of people having to change their schemas – and this always hurts a bit.

If you can get in on the ground floor during start-up, you can try to infuse the heady mix with some security good sense. You will probably find that you can easily fall into two traps: the first is that you will go native, and find it easier to go with the unstructured prototyping flow than defend the security corner; the second is that you will end up playing the part of Cassandra, constantly harping on about doom and gloom, and thereby losing the credibility you will need if you are to be effective over time.

The Ho Chi Minh approach works, but the best thing to bear in mind in this circumstance is how you are perceived. There's nothing like a tight deadline and limited budget to get you to very carefully appraise the true cost benefits of the controls you are proposing. If you can't justify them, then they probably should not be implemented. This is true in all circumstances, but is rarely thrown into sharper focus than in a dotcom start-up.

## NATIONAL SECURITY

National security types have an agenda that is very different from commercial types. My first meeting with government security people was a shock, in that I was forced to ask myself 'do people actually do these things'? These 'things' mostly relate to the 'scheme' by which the UK Government classifies its information. This is called the 'Protective Marking Scheme'. The scheme covers information in all forms and of all types across the UK Government, including national security and defence.

If you are working in such organizations, your only choice is to use the scheme. You can't (officially) get away with anything else. This is one of those rare areas when adherence to the letter of the law is the order of the day.

## PROFESSIONALS

In many organizations there is a core of professionals who are (or who perceive themselves to be) different from everyone else. Examples include the judiciary (judges), doctors, actuaries, probation officers, barristers and teachers. In each of the above examples, I have had experience of people deciding that certain conditions did (or conversely, did not) apply to them. They often demanded a specific set of controls (or exemptions) because they were a special case. In many circumstances this was true, but in many others it was essentially an ongoing attempt to differentiate themselves from the hoi polloi.

In some life insurance companies, the majority of the senior management team consists of Fellows of the Faculty of Actuaries (FFA). There is no doubt that such fellowship is extremely important, as it contains the base knowledge required to run big insurance concerns – I just cannot rid myself of the suspicion that the body will essentially become self-selecting, and lose the vitality and cross-fertilisation that diversity brings. Whatever the case, FFAs are a body who often feel they require custom treatment. The same could be said of dealers within investment banks. They earn the company (and themselves) the big bucks, so why should some seemingly petty bureaucratic practice (like security) get in the way?

Such differentiation is an important element of the 'psychological income' that many people obtain from their work.

## SECURITY DESPOT

The reasons that cause people to choose particular paths in life vary. I chose information security because it looked interesting and new, and I liked the person who ran the department.

There is no doubt that some people choose security for the wrong reasons. They like the idea of control (see Dixon's *On the Psychology of Military Incompetence* regarding authoritarian personalities to understand how negative the effects of this can be). The same applies to many areas of expertise, in that many people join the police or the army for similar reasons. A despotic security person (often displaying authoritarian traits) can become a real problem, especially if you are trying to apply appropriate levels of security rather than apply a standard in its entirety.

Indeed, a resolute determination that every part of a standard should be applied can be counterproductive. If people cannot relate to a control, they will go around it if they can. The entire practice of information security can fall into disrepute. If you recognize a despot, or have to clean up after one, the best approach is to ensure that the control set in place is appropriate. If changes are required (and they probably are), you have to engage your audience as closely as you can. This may mean you are at odds with the despot – this strikes me as inevitable. Despotism, in all its forms, has to be opposed.

## SUMMARY

There are a number of relatively simple steps you can take to address the issue of culture. As with every other comment or suggestion in this book, *there are no magic bullets*. Given that the stepped method used in this book starts with managing by fact, I can only recommend the same. Therefore you need to establish the type of culture you are dealing with – this is sometimes referred to as knowing your enemy.

Identifying cultural types is not straightforward. There are so many aspects to it that the generic models such as those put forward by Hofstede will only take you so far. It does provide a framework, especially if you are trying to make comparisons between different organizations.

Some cultural elements can be measured, but most information needs to be gathered informally. Another stepped approach using the following structure can prove useful. You should analyse your target to establish:

- *Ethics/philosophy* – this includes overall views of employees, the way in which the organization relates to their local community, and the manner in which the organization approaches its profit and reward ethic (does it dispense employee shares or similar equity?).

- *Organizational policies* – these can relate to time management (does the company permit flexible hours, home working, 'duvet days'[12] and so on?). Are the approaches to such matters as bullying,

---

12  A 'duvet day' is a day off work that you claim by phoning in early. You are permitted five or so days per year, and you can take them if you have no 'must do' appointments that day. It almost makes having a hangover respectable.

prejudicial behaviour and co-operation established or is there an unwritten culture?

- *Trust climate* – do staff members feel trusted and that their views are appreciated? Do such elements as building layout reflect strict hierarchical relationships and does an open-door policy prevail?

- The above approach will not provide all the answers, but it's a start. Be conscious of culture – consider the following steps:

- Remind yourself that information security policies and other established norms could easily conflict with the schemas most people operate when working.

- Remind your colleagues who work in information security that failure to meet policy may not be because people are stupid or have 'attitude'.

- Listen.

- Listen.

- Listen (I think the point is made)!

Be open in your discussion – the people on the ground know a lot more about the business than you do. There is a method used commonly in Japanese management: if opinions are sought in a meeting, ask the most junior person first. This allows them to provide more truthful information without them having to follow the patterns laid down by a more senior person. This allows the speaker to avoid giving offence and prevents anyone losing face (very important in Japan and similar cultures).

Cultural change takes time; introducing effective change requires slow steady change rather than constant revolution. See Step 3 of the stepped plan concept outlined in the next chapter for more details of changing things incrementally.

# CHAPTER 3

# How Are We Perceived?

I recall joining a merchant bank in the City of London. My first day was given over to induction, and the induction venue was a warm, cosy and almost womblike basement room with high-quality presentation equipment, comfortable seating and was manned by an array of friendly, presentable people from the HR department. They told me all about the history of the bank. They told me about its superb art collection. They told me about the benefits I would receive. All in all, I was feeling pretty good about the situation.

The feeling was dispelled rapidly when, just prior to a coffee break, one of the HR staff made an apology: 'I'm sorry about this, but the next fifteen minute session is given by the IT security people and it's really, really boring.'

I was stunned, in that I had always thought that security was interesting, and that such a presentation should be the highlight of an induction day. I sat through the presentation and looked at the faces of my fellow attendees; it was boring. I thought 'Is this how people perceive me?'

This chapter covers an area that I consider fundamental to information security practice in general – it is not specific to awareness. Nevertheless the way you are perceived in your professional capacity does and will have a huge impact on the way you present your awareness initiatives. Choice of words, the manner in which you present your case and the way on which you assert your beliefs is an area that has had little concentrated attention. The chapter highlights areas of concern, and concludes with a summary of what you can do to reduce the negative impact of how you are perceived, and how you can enhance the positive.

## RISK COMMUNICATION

When faced with difficult circumstances (such as addressing the media during a disaster, crisis or other unwanted event) it has been established that the level of jargon used by professionals of all types actually increases. Peter Sandman, a recognized US authority on risk communication, states:

> *It is still possible for communicators to make the learning easier or harder – and scientists and bureaucrats have acquired a fairly consistent reputation for making it harder. At Three Mile Island, for example, the level of technical jargon was actually higher when the experts were talking to the public and the news media than when they were talking to each other. The transcripts of urgent telephone conversations between nuclear engineers were usually simpler to understand than the transcripts of news conferences. To be sure, jargon is a genuine tool of professional communication, conveying meaning (to those with the requisite training) precisely and concisely. But it also serves as a tool to avoid communication with outsiders, and as a sort of membership badge, a sign of the status difference between the professional and everyone else.[1]*

I think that we in information security are very poor at expressing ourselves, and often find that risks we *know* to be important are ignored because of this. Part of this problem is an inability to express risk in terms that various audiences appreciate. Whilst some commentators deride the poor state of most people's mathematical understanding, much of the problem starts and ends with poor communication.

Some techniques, such as the annual loss expectancy (ALE) have gained credence, particularly in the field of business continuity management, but this credibility is limited, as is the ALE technique itself. See example overleaf.

One of the problems we face is that many people have a tendency to personalize their understanding of risk, and thereby come to spurious conclusions. I have heard the words 'It has not happened here since I've been working here. Why should I worry about it now?' far too often.

As stated above, understanding risk is based on many factors that you will have to deal with. The following sections outline some broad pointers to address this.

I have already established that people perceive risk in what can be perceived as a strange way. They will tolerate massive risks if they are familiar with them and feel they can exert a degree of control, but will shy from small, unfamiliar ones.

---

1    Sandman Peter M, *Explaining Environmental Risk: Dealing with the Public*, TSCA Assistance Office, Office of Toxic Substances, US EPA, Nov. 1986 booklet, pp. 14–25

## Annual Loss Expectancy

Annual loss expectancy (ALE) forms part of a range of techniques that seek to determine the likelihood and extent of losses due to some unwanted event. Likelihood of loss is normally determined by historical data. By working out the likelihood of a risk occurring within a year, you can determine what is known as the annualized rate of occurrence (ARO). Sources of this historical data are many, but for all sorts of reasons, information security is not well served in this area.

Once the ARO has been calculated for a risk, you can relate it to the potential for financial loss associated with the thing (often referred to as an asset) that you are seeking to protect.

The financial value can be worked out by determining the cost of fixing or replacing the asset. For example if a network router were to fail, you would need to replace the actual hardware and pay for the labour to reinstall the device. You may also have to pay the salaries of those people who were unproductive due to the failure.

Once all these factors are determined, you can work out what is sometimes called the single loss expectancy (SLE).

Combining the ARO and the SLE allows you to work out the ALE. A simple formula to illustrate this is:

$$ARO \times SLE = ALE$$

For example, after the Libyan capital Tripoli was bombed in the 1980s on the orders of US President Reagan, many US tourists were put off visiting Europe on the grounds that they would be targeted by terrorists. Some US tour groups started wearing maple leaf and similar Canadian motifs so as to feel safer from attacks. However, statistics suggest that you are much more likely to suffer personal violence in many US cities than in many perceived European trouble spots.

## TACTICS FOR RISK COMMUNICATION

Once you understand some of the issues relating to risk perception, you can try and ensure you do not add fuel to this fire by communicating poorly. First and foremost, people who are concerned about risk act in an emotional manner. Such emotions, often ignored by actuaries and purist risk managers, are understandable and appropriate because we are emotional beings. You have to empathize with your audience if you want to convince them that a particular risk needs addressing (or, conversely, does not need addressing). If you ignore their concerns as irrelevant or silly, your job will instantly become more difficult.

You should adopt the language and metrics used by your audience. If you are talking to a banker, there's little doubt that he will operate in financial terms. If you are talking to an educator, they are likely to talk in terms of student success rates. Examples chosen from one industry will not be as effective if used in another. Local examples tend to make people identify with them. One of the possible reasons that the initial European response to the 2004 tsunami in the Indian Ocean was initially bigger and more rapid than that of North America is that Thailand, Malaysia and the Seychelles are used more frequently as holiday destinations by Europeans than by North Americans. This does not mean that North Americans are in any way less humane or considerate – they simply had less direct experience and knowledge of the locations affected, and reacted accordingly.

---

### To Confuse a Mockingbird

Use illustrations that your target audience will understand.

I recall a conference I had arranged in an Oxfordshire country mansion. One attendee had come over from New York and brought his wife along as they intended to take a brief holiday after the event. I spoke to her asking if she had enjoyed her day (she had been left to her own devices as we discussed BS 7799 of all things). She seemed happy, and asked me about a particular bird she had seen in the grounds. It was striking, black and white and had a harsh cry. I told her 'I reckon it's a magpie'. She added more one piece of information to help me out: 'It's about the same size as a mockingbird.' One problem: I have no idea what a mockingbird looks like, sounds like or how big it is. I was stupid enough to ask in reply 'Is a mockingbird about the same size as a magpie?'

---

Metrics are often misused, especially as so many of us are functionally innumerate. Just what does 'one chance in a million' mean? Techniques such as ALE (see above) are fine, but communicating results requires you to be able to illustrate your figures with something understandable to your audience. One commonly used illustration is 'about the size of a football pitch'. The figure can be used in multiples for example, 'covering an area the size of three football pitches', and works globally, in that soccer, rugby and American football pitches are all about the same size. Height can be illustrated in such units as 'double-decker buses' or a '10-storey building'. The best extreme example of such illustration was used by Bill Bryson in his book *A Short History of Nearly Everything*.[2] When discussing the size of the solar system, he tells readers that if the planet Jupiter was illustrated as the full stop at the end of this sentence, Pluto would be the size of a microbe, and be some 10 metres away from the full stop.

## LANGUAGE USE AND PERCEPTION

Language and its relation to information security awareness are of particular importance when considering how you communicate, and how you are perceived – both as a person and as part of a profession.

### VOCABULARY DOMAINS

There is a linguistic concept called a 'vocabulary domain'. This is the distinct set of terms used within a specific area of expertise. Lawyers have their own, as do doctors. I had a number of terms commonly used within information security analysed, and the reaction of the linguistic professional who assisted me with the analysis was part shock, part mirth.

When you look at some of the words we use, you might be forced to agree.

- authority
- compromise
- control
- deny
- disable
- failure
- permission
- rule
- violation.

There is a theory that many vocabulary domains reflect the social origins of various practices. For example, most of the words associated with the military

2    Bryson B, *A Short History of Nearly Everything*, Transworld Publishers Ltd: London (2003.)

are based on Norman French words. This is because from medieval times the ruling classes in England for some three hundred years spoke a language (Norman French) that was totally separate from the English spoken by the masses. The results are interesting. As an illustration, an Anglo-Saxon called a pig a pig. The Norman lords of the manor called it pork – a word with Norman French roots (also check out cow/beef and sheep/mutton).

The words I have bulleted above are *all* Norman French or Latin in origin. It is also true that the higher up the social scale someone wishes to appear, the higher the incidence of his or her use of words of Norman French and Latin origin. We use terms like 'prevent'. What's wrong with 'stop'? It's shorter and just as good. Perhaps it's because it comes from Old English. Why use the Norman French 'error' when the Old Norse word 'mistake' is as useful?

The point of this is simple. It is very easy to overcomplicate your language, and use terms that have traditionally been used to talk down to people. This trait does not afflict security people alone – professionals of many disciplines do much the same.

## SELF PERCEPTION AND THE POWER OF WORDS

In addition to the above, an information security manager of my acquaintance, a man of considerable non-athletic bulk weighing over 300 pounds, was asked at a dinner party what it was he did for a living. He didn't try to explain much. He just said 'I'm a cyberspace road warrior.' As an exercise in positive thinking, I can think of few better ways of perceiving oneself in these circumstances.

The power of words and perception is undeniable. During various wars, many politicians talk about cleaning out rats' nests of dissidents, equating them to vermin. Also note that just before the Rwandan genocide, Hutu extremists began referring to Tutsis as 'cockroaches'. The Nazis used words (often allied to images) to depict Jewish people in similar ways. Such use of language can help create a climate in which the foulest acts can be performed, with those performing the acts postulating that they are doing what others know must be done, and that what they are doing is right and proper. This is especially so if you are operating in a despotic regime that actually rewards such behaviour.

The best illustration of this is provided by an experiment performed in the 1960s by Stanley Milgram, a psychologist based at Yale:

## Milgram and Authority

Newspaper advertisements offered volunteers $4.50 for an hour's work, to take part in a psychology experiment regarding memory and learning. Respondents (who were in fact the real subjects of the experiment) were met by a white-coated authoritative 'academic' and another person who was presented as another 'volunteer'. The experiment was explained to the subject, who was asked (along with the other volunteer) to draw lots as to who was to be the 'teacher' and who was to be the 'learner'. The experiment was explained as being about the effects of punishment in learning. The subject was allocated the role of teacher; the supposed drawing of lots was rigged, and the other volunteer was actually part of the real experiment.

The learner was strapped into a chair and an electrode attached to their arm. The stern white-coated academic explained that the electrode is attached to an electric current; controllable via a mechanism the subject was to operate.

The subject was told that the shocks will be painful, but will not inflict permanent damage to the learner. The subject was told that they should switch the current on when learners get an answer wrong. For each subsequent wrong response, the subject is asked to crank up the voltage. The learner made numerous errors, and reacted increasingly as the voltage increased. At a certain level, the learner demands to be released. The teacher (the unwitting subject) will, if he or she questions the process, be told 'The experiment requires that you continue' or something similar. At 300 volts, the learner begins to protest very strongly (by screaming), and eventually falls silent.

As many as 60 per cent of subjects were willing (sometimes with some encouragement) to take the apparent voltage level to over 300. Pre-experiment estimates had suggested that only 4 per cent would. The extent to which people will acquiesce to authority (the white-coated authoritative person) shocked everyone, not least the participants. Variants on Milgram's work have confirmed his initial findings. People will respond strongly to perceived authority.

Perhaps we should not be so shocked at some behaviours. Examples of military personnel treating prisoners badly are not a recent, isolated occurrence. Such behaviour has occurred throughout history. One of the prime reasons why people act this way is our natural tendency to obey authority figures, *especially* when the victim is depersonalized (using some of the language and terms outlined above – gook, skinny, fuzzy-wuzzy, Charlie, infidel, round-eye being further examples).

Such language is a subset of culture. It is the manifestation of the ethics, ethos and central tenets of any organization. Torturers may or may not have been following direct orders from their leaders, but they were almost certainly allowed to feel that they were behaving as good followers. Information security professionals have to set their house in order and carefully consider the way they use language. As has been demonstrated, it has a real and profound effect on behaviour.

In addition to some of the terms mentioned above (authority, compromise, control on so on), there are a number of deliberate choices made by the information security profession to change the way the profession is perceived. Take for example the abbreviation CIA. It's no accident that the terms 'confidentiality', 'integrity' and 'availability' are presented in this particular order. I believe the link to the US Central Intelligence Agency's abbreviation is an attempt to enhance the image of the profession. I suggest that 'availability' is by far the most important aspect of the three words (in terms of information security). CIA is an attempt to make ourselves look more interesting! Further terms commonly used within information security include 'penetration testing' and 'the ping of death'. No doubt feminists balk at the first on the grounds that it is misogynist and phallocentric, and I balk at the second – on the grounds that it's rather silly.

## JARGON AND ITS USES (AND ABUSES)

Language use (and misuse) occurs in a number of situations, not least when dealing with crisis conditions.

Many people consider the unencumbered use of jargon as a means to hide bad or unwelcome news. The terms 'bamboozle' or 'blind me with science' have credence, and reflect general distrust of non-standard language. The effects of jargon use can range from alarm and distrust to people 'switching off', actually or metaphorically.

Jargon has its place, in that it is a useful professional communications tool, but misuse is almost always counterproductive. The actual origin of the word refers to the meaningless twittering and chattering of birds. Chaucer uses the word in his *Canterbury Tales* (*The Merchant's Tale*):

> He was al coltish ful of ragerye[3]
>
> And ful of Iargon as a flekked pye[4].

The result of word and jargon misuse is not direct. It is insidious and will impact over time. To avoid twittering like a bird, engendering unintended meaning and presenting an unhelpful self-image, be careful how you present yourself. Consider your audience, and empathize with their needs. Perception is very powerful, and just as risks are perceived in a way that is seemingly less than logical, perception of information security as a whole can have a significant, unhelpful impact.

## A BARRIER, NOT AN ENABLER

In many instances, particularly when dealing with very senior decision makers, information security occupies the same headspace as cleaning, health and safety, HR and staff associations – things that have to be dealt with but are not part of the real reason the decision makers are at work.

Information security gets in the way. Information security professionals are perceived as demanding action and money, neither of which are welcome. Security introduces practices and procedures that slow everybody down. It makes systems fail by introducing technology that interrupts the mainstream. In short, it is perceived as a barrier. The diagram in Figure 3.1 depicts two views of the world based on the way security is treated. The picture on the left shows security as a black box suspended outside the core business. This illustrates how retrofitted security hangs outside the mainstream consciousness of decision makers. The box on the right shows security as an integral, integrated element that forms part of the matrix of the organization. It is this second concept you should be aiming for.

The popular cry by information security is 'We need to become enablers.' But they're not.

Asking people to invest in security is extremely difficult because the returns are rarely the same as those you would get from a standard cost–benefit analysis of a business opportunity. This is because the returns are uncertain, and

---

3    wantonness
4    magpie

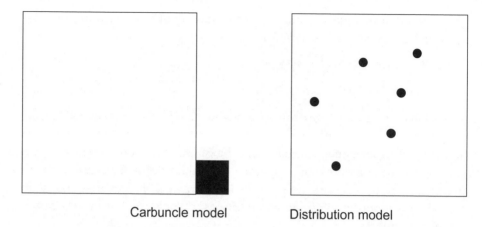

Carbuncle model          Distribution model

**Figure 3.1    Carbuncle/distribution model**

the benefits are measured in events *that have not happened* rather than positive benefits that can be obtained.

To get positive responses to requests for security investment therefore needs a different approach; a risk-based approach is essential. Furthermore, I suspect that risk analysis (or risk assessment) is one of the primary vehicles for delivering good security awareness. I have already alluded to the immediate effectiveness of risk analysis in reducing risk in the 'Designing Out Error' section of the Introduction. I believe that it is the best approach to delivering good awareness, and for permitting us to become enablers.

## SUMMARY

The following points outline suggested actions that will help you manage how you are perceived, and avoid a few potential pitfalls that emerge through use of language:

- Consider how you want to be perceived – what do *you* want to be thought as?

- Whilst a positive self-image may feel good, it is important that whatever you project matches what you can deliver.

- Be aware that emotions are legitimate. Your communications should reflect this and never belittle or deny people's feelings.

- Try to adopt the terminology and vernacular of your intended audience. If addressing an audience with a range of understanding, you must use terms that are clear and informative without being patronizing.

- Examine the language you use. Consider whether there are better alternatives to some of the terms you use habitually.

- Avoid emotive terms and remember the power of words – it is massively misunderstood and underestimated.

- Use jargon sparingly and only in situations when its usage is unambiguous, or when addressing specific audiences who understand the terms used. Remember that some terms can actually be disturbing – I recall the first time an early Windows application told me I had suffered a 'fatal error'. Not very nice and extremely unhelpful.

# *Summary*

You may well recognize and empathize with the issues raised in Part 1. Many of them are generic and occur in many areas outside and beyond information security. As stated in the Introduction Summary, 'Information security awareness is a fundamental part of effective security management. It is not a panacea and requires competence and attention to be paid to a number of parallel activities.'

As these issues are often generic, it is often hard to prescribe a distinct method for dealing with them. Part 2 of this book contains a structured approach to awareness, but the issues raised here in Part 1 have to be borne in mind in all aspects of information security management.

Recognising the human foibles and weaknesses of yourself and others is an important first step. If you assume that sometimes people will make mistakes, and that you create contingency for them, you will eliminate some future pain. One way of avoiding such assumptions is empathy. If you can see an issue from a range of points of view, you are more likely to reduce the number of assumptions you make, and you can also, to some degree, predict and understand others' actions more effectively. This empathy can help you understand why some people come to conclusions that may initially seem illogical and foolish.

Empathy also allows you to understand how people perceive risks. What is vital to some is trivial to others. However infuriating, people will not respond to risk in a cool, logical manner. Risk can evoke emotion, and no dictatorial imposition of control will remove this. The issues raised in Part 1 illustrate how and why this manifests itself. Dealing with risk perception requires you to acknowledge that pure logic and empiricism are not the only answers.

Few things engender more powerful negative emotions than if one is patronized or fed information that is unclear or full of jargon. The manner in which you present yourself is immensely important. Relying entirely on factual content is rarely enough.

Any student of human nature will know how a crisis situation can affect the way people operate. The first thing to go is memory – followed by decision making. The need for clarity and jargon-free communication is never better displayed than in a crisis situation, when the role of human psychology comes very plainly into view.

Psychology is not limited to perception. Further foibles of human nature are manifest in many situations that can lead to poor security decisions. You have to be aware of these, and avoid letting groupthink and other syndromes impact on what you are trying to achieve.

An often seen approach to awareness is the launch of an initiative. Again, human psychology comes into play, in that stepped, incremental change is often more effective than a spectacular launch. Changing your target audience's world view or schema requires empathy and understanding. Incremental change is normally more effective at generating lasting change. A big bang may have a rapid effect, but so often these effects are short-lived.

Allied to incremental change is the development of a positive, rational approach to security. Overly severe application of control (especially if allied to hard-hitting, sudden big-bang change will result in imbalance. Too much control is often as bad as too little. Involving your target audience, seeking their input and commitment allows them to own part of the security initiative. Commitment prevents them from standing aside and ignoring a problem.

Obtaining commitment requires that you understand the culture of the organization you are trying to change. Whilst there are few off-the-shelf tools one can buy to meet the cultural challenge, it is worthwhile trying to work out what culture (or cultures, if you work for a large or dispersed organization) exist. What works in one can fail badly in another. Cultural change is probably the most difficult thing a manager can try and do. Steady, empathetic, incremental change is probably the best solution.

To have an effect on cultural change, it is essential that you consider how you are perceived and how you communicate. If you fail to make a positive impact in your presentation and communications, you will have a more difficult task changing your organization. Bear this in mind, as well as the other considerations presented in Part 1, and the techniques suggested in Part 2 will become markedly more effective.

# *A Framework for Implementation*

CHAPTER 4
# Practical Strategies and Techniques

This chapter does not prescribe a methodology. It sets out ideas and frameworks that can be readily adapted for use in any organization. The framework suggested below is oriented around a stepped approach that incorporates a range of actions.

This chapter also outlines the role that training holds in regard to security awareness. It is a powerful means in itself, but is best used in alliance with other techniques. In addition to this, I have outlined a number of ideas based on a 'guerrilla' approach to security awareness. Sometimes you just have to be pragmatic, and use your resources in the best way possible. The guerrilla approach can give the biggest returns you can find.

## A STEPPED APPROACH

The suggested stepped approach is shown in Figure 4.1.

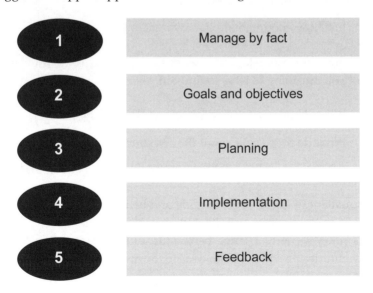

**Figure 4.1    The five-step approach**

The framework is designed to help establish a sustainable, repeatable process. All the steps are interrelated; information gathered in the first step is used to determine goals and objectives in the second. The goals and objectives are used to create metrics and indicators that are central to the fifth.

Another characteristic of the framework is that it is simple. Anybody with the slightest experience in structured project management will recognize it as a simple project management outline.

Note that the steps need not always be performed in the exact order set out here. For example, the development of goals and objectives will often have an impact on the first step. Objectives can drive metrics. The process should be considered as flexible.

## STEP 1 – MANAGING BY FACT

Information security awareness initiatives need to operate this ethic. The managing by fact ethic requires you to ask a series of questions, including:

- Do I need to implement an awareness initiative?

- I've been told to implement an awareness initiative – what should I do?

- How aware are our employees?

- Just how good/bad are our awareness levels?

Whichever question you ask, if you want to be successful in your efforts, at some point you are going to have to find out:

- What do people know (that is, their knowledge)?

- What do they think about the situation (that is, their attitude)?

- What are people actually doing (that is, their behaviour)?

The measurement of knowledge, attitude and behaviour (KAB) is a technique well known in marketing and related disciplines. The main focus of an awareness initiative is to change behaviour, but understanding knowledge levels and attitudes provides guidance as to the most effective means to change behaviour.

Whatever the circumstances of your initiative, obtaining baseline information on the security status of your organization is fundamental. You could, for example, run a survey using a series of questionnaires. Guidance on how this can be carried out effectively is provided in the following chapter, but it is worth looking at this issue here as well.

Empirical information on information security incidents and behaviours is rare and often unreliable. The reasons for this are many, ranging from an understandable reluctance by people and organizations to wash their dirty linen in public, to a lack of thought on the part of practitioners. I have experienced many organizations saying 'Just assume a zero baseline – that we know nothing and have open minds about everything.' There is some sense in this, in that it does not require initial baselining effort (that is we don't have to run upfront surveys and so on), but this does not provide a realistic picture, and could waste a lot of effort, as early initiatives will essentially be untargeted.

In the following paragraphs I suggest a risk-based approach to metrics. I am convinced that this is the way ahead in regard to managing by fact. As empirical evidence is sparse, a well-run risk assessment will provide as a *minimum* the priority order in which awareness issues should be addressed. It may not be able to tell you the total magnitude of the risks involved (and probably never accurately tell you the true extent of potential losses), but it will give the priority order.

Managing by fact is essential; if you don't know what the facts are, you are operating at a disadvantage. One of the primary tools for assessing where and when to invest in security is risk analysis (RA). The various methods include:

- BIA – A business continuity focused methodology

- Cobra – Security risk analysis and BS 7799 compliance software

- CounterMeasures – Risk analysis software

- CRAMM – UK Government preferred method

- RiskPAC – Software that includes some questionnaire design

- RiskWatch – Suite of programmes that covers all aspects of risk

- SARA – Heavyweight analysis approach from the Information Security Forum (ISF)

- SPRINT – Less heavy analysis approach from the ISF.

It is not intended to provide a 'how to' guide for RA in this section. It is intended that the practice can be used to help target your efforts. It is plain that to make the best use of the normally limited funds available, you have to decide where you will provide most benefit. The most beneficial impact you can have is the reduction of information risk.

One fundamental aspect of managing by fact is the identification and classification of your potential audience(s). It is often the case that the funds available for awareness initiatives are limited, and that targeting your efforts will make best use of these funds. In many cases your various audiences will be fairly obvious. In many organizations there are core professionals. An example would be the solicitors in a law firm. They would normally be addressed differently to the more generalist administration staff in the firm. This is partly because they (the solicitors) perceive themselves as different, and because the information they handle (and the laws, rules and regulations that apply) is different.

Identifying target audiences in complex organizations can be made simpler by using a simple grid. Such grids are often used in identifying target audiences for training, and need not be complex to be effective. The factors that go into developing such a grid are varied, but include such elements as:

- grade within the organization (senior, middle and junior management for example)

- job type (professional, administrative and customer facing for example); IT staff often form a specialist audience

- physical location

- country

- language

- ethnicity

- time zone.

It is worth looking at the issues of corporate culture that pertain to this, as this can have a significant impact on the ways and means of delivery, as well as the actual content of the material you are presenting to your various audiences. Such grids can also be used when performing a training needs assessment (TNA) (see the section on TNA below).

A further management by fact fundamental is the need to determine the channels of communication open to you. This involves analysis of the various channels in place (for example, an intranet, a regularly published in-house magazine, regular communication cascades and so on), and then working out if you can use them. It may well be that you have a mature intranet that is well run, but has insignificant impact at the periphery of the organization because of limited connectivity. It is easy from a head office point of view to forget that the services available centrally are much less effective at the edge.

It is also useful at this stage to determine how you can use these channels. There may be people or departments that control these channels. You will need to make sure you know who sanctions what, what lead times apply, and any limitations or constraints (see the box 'Corporate Style Police', below).

---

### Corporate Style Police

In many organizations there exist a group of people whose job is to 'preserve the brand'. Brands are important, in that they are expensive to create, take years to establish, and can be devalued very easily and quickly. The guardians of the brand (the Corporate Style Police) ensure that nothing deviates from the prescribed form. This involves the setting of very specific shapes, fonts, colours and phrases that *must* be used when communicating in print or on screen. These rules normally apply to intranet sites, and are applied with vigour. Before you commit time, money or effort into design, find out about any matters relating to style and branding. Make friends with these people. I have fallen foul of them more than once, and have suffered accordingly. Don't fall into the same trap!

---

## STEP 2 – GOALS AND OBJECTIVES

Most information security awareness initiatives are brought about 'because everyone says I should do one'; few are run on any formal basis. It is a given that without clear goals and objectives, most project-based efforts fail. Step 2 produces such objectives as:

- Ensure all staff are aware of the content of the awareness initiative within six months of commencement.

- Deliver basic training to all relevant staff by year-end.

- Ensure the awareness initiative meets international standard requirements.

There are a number of ways of identifying objectives. These can include:

- relying on internal expertise (sometimes using what is known as a 'Delphic' technique (see below));

- current internal statistics;

- involvement of internal stakeholders;

- risk assessment.

Goals are higher level than objectives, and tend to be fewer in number. A potential goal could be:

> Ensure that all staff know what their personal information security roles and responsibilities are and act accordingly.

or

> Help develop and nurture a security-positive culture in the organization that focuses information security effort on increasing profit by reducing risk.

The main purpose of setting a goal (or goals) and objectives is to *clearly* state why you are taking a particular course of action, and what you want to achieve from it. This provides focus and direction – nothing more.

---

### The Delphic Technique

The Delphic technique is so named after the Oracle of Delphi, a renowned source of knowledge and wisdom in the Ancient Greek world. Delphic techniques involve the gathering of a number of experts in a particular field, and then asking them to provide answers to questions. The final joint answer is then considered the final word on the matter. Some variants use scoring systems, such as providing each potential answer with a score out of ten. The final scores are added up, and the highest scores become the 'correct' answers. The technique becomes flawed if less than five people are involved, or if the chosen 'experts' are not in fact experts.

---

The sections on 'Survey design' and 'Training needs assessment' contain more information and suggestions relating to the definition of goals and objectives.

## STEP 3 – PLANNING

This section is not intended as a guide on how to plan. The suggestions in this section are meant to provide input into an existing, disciplined planning process.

A planning framework should have realistic horizons. I suggest that you can plan in reasonable detail for about three months ahead. Thereafter, the planning details become more generic. A planning cycle of about three years seems about right, in that you can plan the first year using a plan, do, check, act (PDCA) cycle. The advantage of this is that it fits with the ideas set out in ISO/BS 7799. An annual cycle allows you to identify various 'knick points' in your organization's year, such as annual staff conferences.

One reason for taking a three-year view is that the ideas in this book are essentially strategic – corporate change (especially corporate culture change) takes time, and the impact of the changes will not become apparent in a single year. You also have to be able to see the effect you are having on new starters. I have always thought it takes about two years to become truly competent in a job, so you need three years to see if you are having a real effect, otherwise any changes can be attributed to increasing competence rather than a direct result of your efforts.

### Potential techniques

There are a number of well-understood ways by which you can encourage people in your organization to change their behaviour. As stated in the opening chapter, engineering change is, and always has been, difficult. I have always subscribed to the theory that seeking conformity (normally a voluntary action) is a better means for enabling security than seeking compliance (essentially an imposed state). In most organizations, even in strong command-and-control cultures such as the military, imperative demands and exhortation are rarely the most effective means of driving change. Remember that one volunteer is worth twenty pressed men.

The development of a conforming, aware and security positive culture depends on many factors. One is that people will act in a pro-social manner if they themselves feel happy and positive. Bad morale (normally a feature of bad management) decreases positive behaviour, and reduces security. An unhealthy organization is often an insecure organization. Some tactics that can be employed to enhance security are:

- change by increment

- norm of reciprocity

- building a community.

Incremental change is much easier to accept than full-blown fundamental paradigm shifts. Do things a step at a time. Once people get into the habit of accepting your suggested changes, each successive change is a bit easier. This is a tactic that can be used on an ally (or your 'big friend' – see the section below on Guerrilla Techniques), who will then become a catalyst for change for others. It's a bit underhand, but marketing people and politicians have been doing this stuff for years.

One effect of such changes is that people actually change their beliefs (and their attitudes) to conform to their behaviour. It's a form of self-justification – you would think it would work the other way round but apparently not. It is this fundamental psychological trait (known as 'cognitive dissonance') that can form the basis of corporate cultural change. This can be especially effective if backed up by continual positive reinforcement.

The 'norm of reciprocity' is a psychological term that covers that phenomenon when you give someone something (a gift perhaps), this makes the returning of a favour by the recipient more likely. Why else do you think commercial organizations provide giveaways such as promotional badges and mouse mats? It's to make you more likely to return the favour and buy their goods and/or services at some time in the future. I have mentioned before that giveaway items are not central to an awareness campaign, but they are very useful support tools if used sensibly.

Regarding 'building a community', I was once asked to write a regular information security newsletter for a global financial services company. I have plenty of experience writing columns for magazines and writing clear client reports, but was a bit short in editorial experience. I approached the problem by phoning a friend, who happened to be the editor of an international information security magazine and a number of related newsletters. His advice was simple – 'build a community'.

The same principle applies to information security. A community is a group of people who hold something in common. It need not require physical closeness – the Internet shows that communities can exist in cyberspace. What are needed are shared values, shared aims and a common understanding.

Communities can be drawn together by shared experiences – this is why magazines have feedback columns and other means through which people can share. A community centric person will continue to buy the magazine. An information security community can be used (especially if it contains opinion formers and associated big friends) as a further catalyst for change.

If you do publish material (the medium is irrelevant – it could be paper based or on an intranet), then by providing a means for interacting (competitions are very good for this), you can establish and reinforce a community.

One of the main reasons for building a community is to encourage people who had read your material, or visited your intranet site, to do so again. People like interacting with people who have similar interests, so allowing your community to interact with each other provides further adhesion.

The methods for building and retaining a community vary, but can include:

- *Bulletin and message boards.* These should be monitored to stop single interest groups and eccentrics from dominating a theme or conversation. Discussion threads can be powerful means of exchanging useful information (and for gathering useful, if unstructured feedback). There are a number of suppliers of forum and bulletin board software (some of it freeware) that make setting up such channels relatively straightforward.

- *Calendars.* These can range from simple 'forthcoming events' listings to more complex interactive systems. They are useful if you intend developing an events schedule (such as online discussions – see the section below on chat rooms). Do remember that you should keep such calendars up to date. I find few things as annoying as an event listing that contains nothing but lists of events that have already happened.

- *Chat rooms.* Chat rooms have developed a bad name recently, as they are depicted in the news media as places where children are stalked and entrapped. They have a degree of informality when compared to moderated online forums and message boards. They also need moderation, and this can be time consuming if the chat room is used a lot. Someone has to decide when someone is becoming abusive or troublesome.

Many chat rooms developed a schedule as a means of focusing time and attention onto a particular topic on a particular day. Again, software for such facilities is available freely on the Internet.

- *Newsletters.* I have noticed a recent reduction in faith regarding newsletters. Perhaps it's because they are becoming easier to produce (the templates supplied in standard products like MS Word and Publisher make this pretty simple), or maybe it's because people are demanding screen-based information. This reported lack of faith emanates from communications professionals in large corporates, so cannot be ignored. HTML-based e-mail newsletters are now becoming the standard, and given the increasing use of high-speed links, becoming more acceptable to users, even in home environments. What will happen is that newsletters will become smarter, and people will receive them in a customized form created with their individual interests in mind. This is a powerful tool, and cannot be ignored.

A community can be used in a variety of ways. They are a sounding board, an influencing group, a communications channel and a focus group. They are a precious resource, and you should nurture them.

## Force field diagrams

One of the most useful approaches I have seen used to enhance planning is to use a change management technique that focuses on what is called a 'force field diagram'.

This force field concept is based on the accepted theories of Kurt Lewin, a psychologist who developed a range of social psychology fundamentals in the 1920s and 1930s.

Kurt Lewin[1] (1890–1947) was a social psychologist whose extensive work covered studies of leadership styles and their effects, work on group decision making, the development of force field theory, the unfreeze/change/refreeze change management model, the 'action research' approach to research, and

---

1    Lewin K, *The Methods of Kurt Lewin, A Study of Action and Effect* (1929).

the group dynamics approach to training. Lewin has had a great influence on research and thinking on organizational development, and was behind the founding of the Center for Group Dynamics in the United States, through which many famous management thinkers passed. Lewin is best known for developing Force Field Analysis, using Force Field Diagrams. The classic force field diagram helps a group picture the tug-of-war between forces around a given issue, such as behaviour relating to information security. A force field diagram is depicted in Figure 4.2.

The theory pays particular attention to enabling change through identifying and eliminating restraining forces. Effort spent on increasing a driving force can make a significant difference, but in order to maintain the effect, the force has to be maintained. An example of such an effort would be increasing police effort to detect and prosecute drink driving.

Using the following steps can radically enhance your plans:

1.  Identify the driving and restraining forces.

2.  Identify the key (restraining) forces.

3.  Identify appropriate action steps (for removing restraining forces).

4.  Review and evaluate action steps.

The identification of the driving and restraining forces is fundamental to the approach. Making a longer-term change is normally more time and cost-effective

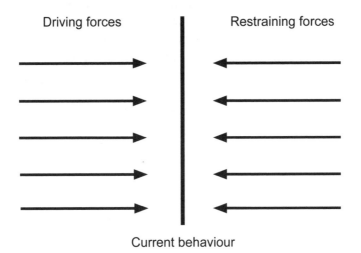

Driving forces        Restraining forces

Current behaviour

**Figure 4.2     Force field diagram**

if the restraining force is identified and changed appropriately. Continuing the example of drink driving mentioned above, the thing with the greatest effect in reducing drink-driving offences in recent years in the UK has been the changing of public perception of drink driving from being a minor offence to being a serious social crime. People now report people suspected of driving under the influence. Publicans and others physically prevent people from driving off by taking their car keys. Although punishments and police efforts have increased, the restraining force of relatively benign public acceptance of driving whilst drunk has been replaced, and the change in behaviour is very apparent. The other parts within the process can form a key element within a plan.

An example of a restraining force is what is termed 'over-control'. If you have a very strict password usage procedure and process that demands many characters of mixed types be used when creating a password, you run the risk of making the process so demanding that people will do a number of things. They may start:

- writing passwords down on post-it notes and leaving them on their screens;

- sharing passwords to avoid multiple changes;

- start bad-mouthing the security department.

Whichever of the actions they take, they are the unintended reaction to over-control. Removing the restraining force need not compromise security. You could develop a simple single sign-on process, removing the need for multiple passwords. You could introduce a token-based solution, again removing the need for a good memory. What is important is that the solution has to make your charges' lives easier without compromising security. It could be suggested that over-control can actually decrease security *and* bring you and your department into disrepute.

A major aspect of planning is to work out how you want to measure the effectiveness of your initiative. You need realistic metrics; Chapter 5 'Measuring Awareness' provides guidance on this matter in more depth . It is normally useful at a late stage in the planning process to take stock and make sure there is a sensible relationship between goals, objectives, metrics and forces (driving and restraining), and that they form a reasonably contiguous whole. The restraining forces relate to behaviours the initiative is designed to change. These should form the basis of the initiative metrics, which in themselves should meet the objectives. If they don't, the initiative metrics will not let you know if you have reached your objectives. The three elements have to line up. Some people like to include other aspects to this range of concepts, such as 'critical success factors'. If you are comfortable with such concepts, they can form a useful addition to your planning / implementation process.

## STEP 4 – IMPLEMENTATION

Implementation need not involve a high-profile launch – it can be low key. Indeed, given that changing people by increment is sensible, avoiding a big-bang approach can be the most effective approach. The most important thing to remember is that people can suffer from 'initiative fatigue'. If people are constantly deluged by health, safety, quality, diversity and regulatory initiatives, they will eventually begin to ignore them. The natural human response to such overload is 'What pointless activity do they want me to take part in now?' People sometimes see initiatives as 'those silly things I have to do rather than doing productive work'. If you are deluged at work, why do you think you can use the same techniques for security?

Your implementation plan should be decided in the planning stage, and it should always reflect the environment it's supposed to operate in.

You can do a big bang (coordinated combinations of articles in in-house publications, e-mail blitzes to 'everybody@company', a 'meet and greet' at reception during the morning rush and a web broadcast on the intranet), but overkill will desensitize your audience. I thought I was doing the right thing when I appeared in a monthly in-house magazine four months running (announcing the initiative, presenting a competition, announcing the winners then presenting the cheque), but feedback suggested otherwise. People were sick of my logo, my damnable fluffy bugs and me.

Operating by stealth gets round this issue. One of the reasons that people want to have a fairly rapid effect is that they are often judged (that is they have their work performance appraisals) on an annual basis. Corporate change is a strategic issue, and cannot be seen in what is a short timescale. A tactic to get round this appraisal issue is to ensure you have included some early wins into your plan, and that you can be seen (and perceived) as having moved forward in the first year. In addition to this, over-optimistic planning can lead you to seek unrealistic achievements (such as the whole company becoming totally aware in one year) that will impact the entire programme when you fail to meet them.

## STEP 5 – FEEDBACK

If you have developed your metrics sensibly your feedback should give you guidance on how well the initiative is being received, and how effective it is in meeting your objectives. Given that the emphasis in this book is on changing behaviour, the most important and most empirical measures should relate to specific behaviours.

If you have successfully developed an information security community, these people can also provide excellent feedback.[2]

It is important to remember that when you make an overtly public statement, such as setting out an awareness initiative, some people will make a strong public display of attacking whatever you present. This will happen no matter the quality of your material, no matter the elegance of your text, no matter the integrity of your audience analysis. You cannot please all of the people all of the time. There's something about making a public statement that causes some people to feel they are art critics, expert copy-editors and time-served graphic designers. Ignore them and keep the faith. Life's too short.

## TRAINING

Training covers a multitude of techniques, ranging from face-to-face encounters to sophisticated computer-based training (CBT) modules. Each approach has pros and cons – most of which centre on time availability and cost.

What is important to remember is that adults learn new things in a way that is very different from the manner in which children do. Adults have a very strong idea of 'self', and come equipped with memories, experiences and prejudices. To make training (and therefore learning) effective, these issues have to be borne in mind. An adult needs to be willing to learn, and making the learning process relate to the learner's knowledge and understanding is essential. If you can imbue the proceedings with a perception of value, the learner will be much more willing. This book takes a fairly strong Theory Y/conformity stance and this approach seems to be supported in most of the literature on adult learning. Forcing an employee to undertake training for which they hold little perceived value, can't relate to, and feel no ownership

---

2    Remember that your community may well consist of people who have knowledge of or a vested interest in security. Their feedback, whilst undoubtedly useful, will be biased by these factors. Empirical feedback comes from disinterested people.

for will make them generally unwilling to learn. This will significantly reduce your effectiveness.

When drawing various diagrams and mindmaps during the process of writing this chapter, one word kept occurring and reoccurring – involvement. To paraphrase Confucius 'Tell them and they might listen, demonstrate and they might learn, *involve* them and they will understand.'

Involving your audience is essential, and using their input will help identify training needs and may shape the design of the programme itself. Another theme in this book is the implementation of change; training is designed to increase knowledge, change attitudes and induce changes in behaviour (remember the KAB acronym). If people think they have some control over this change they are more likely to accept the results. Not having control is one of the prime sources of personal stress and can even become threatening to individuals.

Other factors that help this learning process include motivation. Adults in particular must *want* to learn. The learning should be relevant and be in the personal interest of the learners. Adults (and children) often benefit from a combination of sight and sound. Audio-visual media can be very effective. Face-to-face presentations (using the ubiquitous PowerPoint) use this technique (although beware of 'death by PowerPoint' by overusing bulleted slides). Modern CBT modules can be developed that incorporate voice, and this is very effective. This can increase comprehension should your audience normally speak another language . Other factors, such as poor literacy can make the use of voice-overs extremely beneficial.

One of the most powerful training reinforcement mechanisms involves asking participants to practise whatever it is you are asking them to do as part of the training process. These can range from role-play to handling software, applying physical techniques or indulging in problem-solving activities. These techniques are often presented in breakout sessions away from the normal training room. This provides breaks in the training process (people hate to sit in one room all day being talked at).

If adults cannot relate to what they're being taught, they will find it more difficult to learn. This characteristic of learning reflects my understanding of the use of examples in presentations. I hear many people use examples (perhaps of disasters) that are very distant from the audience experience. If you were schooled, employed and continue to live in the UK, examples of disasters from Japan will mean rather less than a local example. Distance and irrelevance can induce the 'won't happen here' syndrome that so often kicks in if groupthink begins to manifest. It also reflects the Fischhoff, Slovic and Lichtenstein view regarding the familiar and unfamiliar (see 'Perception of Risk' in Chapter 1).

The establishment of training objectives that are stated and understood by the intended audience can make learning easier, in that the audience should (if the objectives are well crafted and clearly stated) feel they could participate. If they know what it's for, why they're doing it and feel they've been involved, the chance of successful training increases substantially. People also appreciate feedback on their performance!

One of the most effective techniques I use when learning is to write down a précis (sometimes using bullet points) of what is delivered to me in training sessions. The act of analysing and writing the words helps to reinforce the key points – some people call this 'internalising'. Such learning can be done through breakout discussion groups but practical exercises can be extremely effective as well.

## TRAINING EVALUATION

Donald L Kirkpatrick, a former national president of the American Society for Training and Development, developed what has become a classic framework for evaluating training[3]. These four levels of evaluation are:

- reactions

- learning

- job

- organization.

Each successive evaluation level is built on information provided by the lower level. According to the Kirkpatrick model, evaluation should start with the lowest level and then move sequentially through the higher levels. This succession provides an increasingly detailed, granular analysis of the effectiveness of the training, although each higher level requires additional time and effort (and therefore, budget).

---

3   Kirkpatrick D L, *Evaluating Training Programs: the four levels*, Berrett-Koehler: San Francisco (1994).

## Level 1 evaluation – reactions

Evaluation at this level measures the reactions of target audiences to the provided training. It tries to answer questions relating to trainee perceptions of the material in question: Did they enjoy it? Was it relevant? Some people refer to Level 1 evaluation as a 'smilesheet'. Every programme should, as an absolute minimum, be evaluated to this level. The comments and information received can be used to improve the training programme (smilesheets are very good at pointing out the obvious – something that's often missed by the supposed experts!).

## Level 2 evaluation – learning

Level 2 takes the process well beyond assessing student happiness and satisfaction. It is at this level that one can begin assessing knowledge and attitude (see Step 1 in the 'Stepped approach' earlier in this chapter). The training evaluation levels equate well with the KAB model. To determine effectiveness, you need to start from an understanding of base information. Therefore Level 2 sometimes needs a degree of pre-testing to determine the base from which students are working. After training, students are then required to undergo a post-test phase.

## Level 3 evaluation – job

This level is sometimes referred to as 'Transfer'- as it attempts to measure the change that has occurred in student behaviour. The level equates to the 'B' in the KAB model. In truth, it is this measurement that is the most important of all, as increased knowledge and a better attitude don't matter if there has been no positive behavioural change.

Measuring behaviour is difficult, but it is as close to empiricism that we in information security management get.

## Level 4 evaluation – organization

This level seeks to determine the effect the training has had at the highest level. In a commercial organization we would hope to see increased profits (or decreased losses). The actual result depends on the objectives you have set yourself in your programme. They could include:

- reduction in downtime

- increase in reported incidents

- reduction in reporting time during incidents
- reduction in insurance premium levels
- reduction in the number of 'dead' user IDs.

## TRAINING NEEDS ASSESSMENT

Training needs assessment (TNA) is a process that indicates what training is required for whom. The analysis matches your potential target population against current and required knowledge and skill. Knowledge or understanding on the part of an individual can be expressed as:

- zero knowledge;
- low-level awareness of standard terminology;
- low-level knowledge of subject matter (normally gained informally);
- low-level understanding of subject matter (including some theory) normally gained via a formal learning channel; for example, training;
- some practical application of subject matter supported by formal training (perhaps up to one year's experience);
- sound practical application of subject matter supported by formal training (one to two years' experience);
- prolonged practical application supported by a formally recognized professional or academic qualification (more than two years);
- recognized industry expert with ability to provide consultative advice and/or training in the subject.

The establishment of training needs that are directly related to clearly defined objectives is a fundamental requirement. These objectives should be established as part of the broader stepped approach described earlier. Establishing training needs are much the same as establishing awareness programme objectives. The emphasis should be on a problem that needs to be addressed or a risk that needs to be mitigated.

Just as with the stepped approach, there are other drivers that direct a needs assessment. These can include:

- standards compliance

- legislative pressure

- audit points.

A TNA can identify shortcomings in standards compliance or other (normally external) requirements that can be addressed wholly or in part by training.

It is worth outlining the established methods and terminology used when performing a TNA. A structured approach to TNA includes a number of logical steps. These could include:

- issue identification

- analysis

- identification of training needs.

## Issue identification

The following points can identify issues that are likely to be appropriately addressed by structured training:

- *Incidents*: Issues can be drawn out by analysis of event logs and incident reports. Whilst the lack of plentiful, truly empirical data on information security incidents is well known, what information that does exist at a local level can provide a useful starting point. Other evidence can include legal actions, negative relations with regulatory bodies (including actual regulation compliance failures) and critical system outages (such as power and UPS failures, and network and application collapses).

- *Foreseen risks*: Risks can be identified before they manifest. Examples include new technology developments, office moves, environmental changes, business process re-engineering and organizational mergers.

- *Regulatory requirements*: New regulation (such as required practices demanded by the UK Financial Services Authority) can be anticipated and factored into TNA. The development (or organizational acceptance of) new standards (ISO 17799 for example) can also be anticipated, and the relevant TNA carried out.

### Analysis

Once the issues have been identified, further analysis helps determine the training needed to meet them. The analysis should concentrate on the effectiveness of people, teams and processes. Analytical questions could include:

- What is actually meant to be happening?

- Are there standards that are not being met?

- Why is this happening?

When researching the book I noticed that there are many other researchers who have determined that involving participants in most activities (training, awareness, education and so on) at an early stage increases the effectiveness of that activity. This is valid *even when the person involved does not personally agree with the way the activity is managed.* The key element is involvement. When identifying training needs, you will be more effective if you obtain low-level feedback from your target audience.

Obtaining this feedback can provide an opportunity to assess skill and knowledge levels. You can use the opportunity to identify if particular individuals require additional assistance, or if training content is appropriate. This is important in cases when candidates are perhaps borderline, or if there are specific issues relating to literacy and numeracy.

One major aspect of TNA is that at some point you need to understand the priority order in which training should be delivered. Your starting point should be the areas where the lack of training could produce severe negative impacts. It is possible that upfront risk analysis will have provided the relative priority, but if this is not available, an understanding of potential consequences provides a simple but effective guide.

Just as with the objectives set out in Step 2 of the stepped approach described above, training objectives can help target your efforts by defining appropriate content and the delivery mechanisms. As objectives describe what it is you want to achieve, they should be quite specific. For example, a training objective could be 'To ensure that all employees know where to find information about security issues,' or 'All new entrants since January have undergone, and understand, security induction training.'

## Identification of training needs

There are a number of methods that can be used to determine training needs. Your choice will depend on your local conditions. The following ideas should be regarded in conjunction with those set out in Step 2 of the stepped approach. Examples include:

- review of policy and related documents

- event analysis

- interviews

- direct observations

- survey and related data gathering.

All of the above can be used singly or in conjunction with each other. Document review is useful in determining corporate aspirations. It's important to remember that writing a policy is easy – but to implement one is very difficult. With this in mind, a policy and document review will only reveal part of the picture. In line with the key message of this book, it is behaviour that is paramount, not intent.

Event analysis is the closest we can get to empirical analysis. Events tend to be behaviour driven, and information on real events that are well recorded can be used to target your efforts accurately. As said before, such information is rare and almost never well recorded. If you want to manage by fact, you will probably have to set such recording mechanisms yourself. Event recording can be facilitated by software that is often found in larger IT installations, such as Remedy, but these need to be supported by carefully designed processes to ensure the output gained is what is wanted. Logs from servers and network devices contain a hoard of incident and status data that is rarely well used. The main reason for this is that different logs use different formats, and the volume of information is vast. This makes useful analysis of the data complex and time consuming. Research by the SANS Institute[4] suggests that some 73 per cent of large global companies destroyed their logs after a year, and that 33 per cent kept data for less then a week. Event analysis is not easy.

Interviews are useful for a number of reasons. Many of these are also discussed in 'Measuring Tools and Techniques' in Chapter 5, but I will outline them here. Face-to-face interviews are expensive (because they take time), but

---

4   http://isc.sans.org/poll.php?pollid=35&results=Y.

**Event Logs**

There are a growing number of solutions available to help in the gathering and analysis of log data. The processes involved focus on the following terms:

*Collection*: Modern systems can produce large volumes of log data. It's easy to become bogged down in this volume, or fail to collect valuable but volatile data that normally exists in short term memory. Intelligent analysis of what you want the data to tell you can help determine what you collect and how long you store it for.

*Normalization*: Just about every type of log data is stored in a different form. Normalization is the process wherein data is formatted into a common form. Date and time information can be transformed into a common format (using a single time zone for example, such as GMT).

*Aggregation*: Like normalization, aggregation combines data from multiple sources, and sets them in a form whereby a wider view of an event can be taken (looking at a system as a whole rather than a single device or example).

*Correlation*: This process seeks connections between seemingly separate events using normalized, aggregated data. This allows investigations into events that have potentially multiple causes, or when the evidence for the event has previously existed in disparate forms and locations.

*Analysis*: This is the process (often supported by event logging and management software) that determines actions after an event. This can be assisted by automated alarm processes that indicate the likelihood of an event happening using mathematical heuristics and predetermined benchmark levels. These act as triggers for an alarm.

you can gather a lot of what some call 'side-band' information from gestures and body language. You can use these cues to investigate areas that could be deemed 'off script'. The value of these diversions is hard to quantify, but can be huge; I always seem to say 'I never knew that' at some point during interviews. You can interview over the phone (see Chapter 5 again) and retain some of the value of feedback and diversion, but you lose the subtle body language and gesture feedback.

Direct observation is a bit like event data. It is empirical (well, as close as damn it) provided you are recording distinct events. It is limited by the number of observers, but can be used to gauge mood and similar elements that are hard to quantify.

## TRAINER SELECTION AND INSTRUCTIONAL METHODS

When selecting a trainer, especially in a specialist area such as information security, you have to consider two factors – teaching ability and subject knowledge. If you are confident you have people who combine both, you are lucky. Subject knowledge is often deemed easier to obtain than teaching ability. The problem with having a specialist teacher delivering subject matter that they are not expert in is that they often find it hard to deal with questions that take them off script. If you are teaching an audience with specialist skills, they often delight in exposing a teacher's weaknesses.

Natural teaching ability is rare. You can be trained to be competent, but the deep-seated ability to communicate cannot. You have to match your choice with your expected target audience, and with the objectives you have chosen. If a knowledgeable, belligerent crowd of technical experts confronts you, it may be best to establish up front that you are passing on generic messages, and that you are not an expert yourself. Pretending you are will expose you should they twig that you're bluffing!

One factor that is often overlooked is scheduling. Any information security training you deliver will, for the most part, be regarded by your audience as outside their mainstream work. You should seek to minimize disruption, and also make sure you don't try too much at once. I have endured two-hour lectures from deadly dull subject experts who had little teaching ability. Suffice to say, I can't remember a thing about the subject – I can only recall that beards, checked shirts and orange ties do not go well together.

The choice of training method is driven by a number of factors. These normally include:

- channels currently available

- geography

- your objectives

- audience location and distribution

- your timescales.

The types of methods available include lectures, seminars, CBT modules, online video streaming and subtle combinations of all of them. One such combination is referred to as a 'webinar' (a two-way seminar that is conducted over the Internet). There are techniques involved that can be incorporated into many of these channels. These include role-play, 'break-out' sessions that involve problem-solving exercises and group discussions. If you are dealing with a dispersed audience working in multiple small units, a CBT delivered via a standard desktop may prove cost effective. A one-man road show of lectures between multiple sites may work, provided you are not pushed for time.

It is important to remember that adults learn best if they are taught via a combination of media (sight and sound for example). It is also essential to understand that there may be different levels of learning required, and that these levels (linked to Kirkpatrick's levels of evaluation) may require the use of different channels and media.

It is advisable to test the efficacy of your chosen teachers, media and methods before going live. Early involvement with representatives of your target audience will engage them, provide feedback that can be tested against your evaluation criteria, and give you a chance to assess your teachers. There is nothing like a disinterested view of your offerings to highlight your shortcomings.

Just as pre-testing is fundamental, you have to consider how you are going to manage the effects of training *after* you have delivered it. Just as adults learn best through multiple channels, learning is reinforced by a degree of repetition after the event. Follow-up forms (ideally sent within ten days of the training finishing) can be used to highlight the key messages you wanted attendees to learn or understand. You can also obtain retrospective feedback. This is often different from what you receive immediately after a training session, as attendees have had time to reflect and digest the training subject content.

## COMPUTER-BASED TRAINING

For many years computer-based training (CBT) has had a mixed reception by information security professionals. From my early professional days I remember CBT modules as stilted and dull. I used to defeat the monotony by breaking out of the CBT module and playing with the computer operating system.

Some high level research was undertaken in the early 1990s by a group of information security managers who were employed by various London-based investment banks. They used the 'Delphic' technique: they listed their personal favourites in priority order of various awareness media, and these were then aggregated to give an expert view of their *perceived* effectiveness. The results ranked CBT amongst the lowest of all education media. I suspect that they, like me, had been subjected to dull 'press the space bar to continue' CBT modules of the worst DOS-based kind.

Things have changed. The increased power of current workstations, and the incorporation of sound, graphics and interaction into CBT modules have made them much more interesting, powerful and flexible. They can also be used in conjunction with web-based technology, allowing them to be incorporated into intranets. Furthermore, the user/student actions taken and other interactions can be recorded and used as a means to track respondent knowledge, attitude and behaviour. In short, we now have a vehicle for awareness dissemination, reinforcement and tracking all in a single implementation.

Whilst this may seem a panacea, it is not. It is still very easy to present bad material using good technology. You still have to do the basics – a poorly planned, badly written, patronizing awareness initiative will remain just so regardless of the presentation medium used (see 'Media effectiveness' in Chapter 6).

Keeping track of student progress via modern CBT solutions can provide you with an understanding of the training status of the organization. Examples of these types of deliverable include:

- a reported module (confirming that a particular person has accessed the training module)

- a tested course (only permitting users to continue after a correct answer is given)

- an examined course (normally using multiple choice questions).

All the above can be used separately or together, depending on the target audience make-up and the objectives of the training. The data gathered from such CBT modules can be recorded in many simple forms. I have seen solutions that generate comma separated value (CSV) data that can be downloaded directly into commonplace tools such as Microsoft Excel. I have also seen more complex arrangements that download data to sizeable databases to be accessed via Structured Query Language (SQL). The type of recording and analysis method chosen depends on the purpose and scale of the training need the CBT module seeks to address.

## QUALIFICATIONS

Information security has seen a growth in professional qualifications over the last few years. These include:

### BCS ISEB Certificate in Information Security Management Principles

The British Computer Society (BCS) Information Systems Examination Board (ISEB) Certificate in Information Security Management Principles is designed to provide assurance that the holder has a fundamental foundation of knowledge necessary to undertake information security responsibilities as part of their normal job, or who are thinking of moving into information security or an information security related function.

Taking (and passing) the examination provides an opportunity for those already within an information security management role to enhance or refresh their knowledge and in the process gain an industry recognized qualification that provides *demonstrable* assurance of the holder's level of profession specific knowledge.

The Certificate is awarded after a two-hour examination that requires the student to answer 100 multiple-choice questions (there are four options offered on an answer sheet designed for optical reading and automated marking). The answers offered normally have two choices that are well off the mark, then two that are closer contenders. Some of the options seem to *all* be correct. I remember four colleagues discussing an ISEB paper they had just sat. All four had answered the same question differently, and all could present cogent reasons for their choice. I recall thinking 'well… it depends' on several occasions when sitting the exam. The trick seems to be to try and work out what the examiner *wants* the answer to be rather than trying to establish the professionally *correct* answer; it is possible that there is a degree of cultural loading in the question set.

### CISM

CISM (Certified Information Security Manager) is a qualification offered via the Information Security and Control Association (ISACA). ISACA is a professional body that represents (for the most part) IT Auditors. It is descended from the Electronic Data Processing Auditors Association (EDPAA), a name that betrays its age and lineage. CISM is designed to meet the professional qualification aspirations of experienced information security managers and others that may have information security management responsibilities. CISM is designed to provide senior management with assurance that those passing the examination have the required knowledge and the capacity to provide effective security management and effective information security consulting. CISM is business focused, concentrating on information risk management whilst addressing management, design and technical security issues at a fairly high conceptual level. CISM is designed to be of benefit to those in the information management field who perform security work, but perhaps do not focus entirely on it.

## CISSP

A Certified Information System Security Professional (CISSP) is a qualification for more technical information systems security practitioners. The CISSP examination comprises some 250 multiple-choice questions, covering topics that include:

- access control systems

- cryptography

- security management.

The CISSP qualification is managed by the International Information Systems Security Certification Consortium – known as (ISC)$^2$. (ISC)$^2$ promotes (indeed, markets) the CISSP exam as 'an aid to evaluating personnel performing information security functions'. CISSP is becoming a required qualification in many parts of the world (notably the US). I am aware of certain organizations that demand CISSP for all information security staff, irrespective of true role and grade. CISSP alumni can make use of a web portal (CISSP.com) designed to 'promote the CISSP Certification, share knowledge and communication amongst certified information system security professionals and is an information service website to help information security professionals who are seeking to become CISSPs'.

I am aware of historic concern that CISSP was 'too American' for European circumstances, but I am also aware of considerable efforts to correct this and make the examination less culturally loaded. Some commentators question the extremely technical nature of much of the syllabus content. It is possible that some candidates may, if concerned about CISSP content, be better suited to the CISM qualification. There is no doubt that CISSP is much more widely accepted at the time of going to press.

# GUERRILLA TECHNIQUES

One of the biggest mistakes some information security practitioners make is failing to appreciate that their perceptions about the critical importance of information security are not necessarily shared to the same degree as other people in the organization. The trick, rather than tub-thumping, is to win the hearts and minds of the workforce. Given that there only tiny resources available, you have to beg, steal or borrow to get heard. There are a series of guerrilla techniques you can use to help in this task:

- get a big friend;
- make friends with HR;
- work with your local auditors;
- piggyback, hijack and cadge.

## GET A BIG FRIEND

Having someone at senior (maybe board) level that understands information security and is sympathetic to your requirements is manna from heaven. This is especially so if your big friend is considered an opinion setter and a leader.

Treat your big friend well – avoid upsetting them. Investing your time and effort in cultivating an effective big friend will pay dividends; this involves spending time communicating (and listening to them), sharing successes as well as potential threats and problems. A board-level champion will influence others and may help gain access to funds, time and people to help you carry your message out across the organization.

## MAKE FRIENDS WITH HR

Human resources (HR) have a number of similarities to information security, in that they are often group functions, have an appetite for producing policies and other imperatively drafted documents, and are routinely required to communicate with broad swathes of employees across the organization.

This communication capability is something information security can use. The best example of such use I remember was an annual staff attitude survey. HR ran the survey, which was designed by proven marketing professionals and recorded in proven reporting software. I managed to place four information security questions into the survey, which was sent to all staff across a UK-wide organization. It hit a population of about 40 000 respondents, and taking part was mandatory. These four questions produced the most comprehensive data I have ever had on user attitudes to security. The respondent detail included age, job type, gender, physical location, department and grade. Such rich information was a gold mine, and it was repeated every year.

HR departments also tend to either house or have good relationships with other departments such as corporate communications. These departments can be incredibly useful, especially if they have a graphic design function. As these people are often in charge of such things as corporate identity, they can be extremely useful when it comes to putting together professional-looking awareness initiatives (which conform to internal style rules). Make friends with these people too.

## WORK WITH YOUR LOCAL AUDITORS

Be nice to auditors. They often have an abundance of skills, and an impressive back-catalogue of audit reports which are filled with all sorts of facts, network diagrams, analysis and sundry other useful material. These reports can be really useful when preparing a risk-analysis exercise, in that you can come into an interview already primed.

Traditionally auditors have been depicted as aggressive and unhelpful – they are trying very hard to change this, and are behaving in a much friendlier way. Also note that you can use them as a lever to change people's minds. If you can convince someone that doing what you say will get the auditors off their backs, it's amazing how quickly they'll jump.

## PIGGYBACK, HIJACK AND CADGE

As guerrillas, you rarely have access to the kind of funds you need. This means you should make do and mend and take advantage of opportunities to work through others. Examples include:

### Cascade meetings

These are sometimes termed 'communications' meetings, and are normally held at regular intervals (perhaps weekly). Cascade meetings are structured forums designed to pass corporate information down through the ranks to make sure everybody is 'on message'. If you can get your ideas, material or name sent through these channels, you can hit almost 100 per cent of your potential audience. Do remember that these meetings run the risk of being about as interesting as a train timetable to attendees. The challenge is to be imaginative if you want to stand out, catch their attention and encourage them to change their behaviour.

### Weekly intranet news broadcasts

Many companies have a weekly e-mail broadcast of corporate news, often including financial information, performance and acquisition news, as well as HR warnings and so on. You can use such events to promulgate any hot issues you want to air. Using such channels also makes sure that the message is seen as 'mainstream'.

## OTHER CORPORATE INITIATIVES

There are many similarities between various functions within an organization that act corporately. These include health and safety, quality and HR. These functions can be a double-edged sword for information security. You may find that you are categorized with them, and this can make communicating your message harder, as busy people often lump such non-core items together, and try to ignore them collectively. The upside is that you can borrow a ride on their initiatives, and make use of their communications channels, material, time and effort. In an effort to avoid being dragged into politics, acting in a co-operative manner in your dealings with fellow corporate bodies can help shape an affiliative culture. Behaviour breeds culture, so 'walking the talk' in this manner will bring long-term benefits, even if there may be perceived short-term costs.

## SUMMARY

Incremental change is normally the most effective way of creating and maintaining change. Taking a measured, targeted approach allows you to take such an approach. Information security awareness has to operate within a structure that provides measures and targets if it is to be demonstrably effective. There are many means by which this can be achieved, but I advise strongly that your first action should be to consider *what* it is you want to do well before you consider *how* you're going to do it.

The five-step approach set out in this chapter can be linked to a number of techniques, not least the development of targeted training. Training needs assessments and suitable evaluation can be easily integrated into the five steps. Just as the five-step approach should initially consider what it is you want to achieve, training techniques must do the same. It is easy to be seduced by the visual and audio attractions of technology, not least the new types of computer-based training modules that are now available. You have to remember that effectiveness will be enhanced by dealing with your requirements prior to choosing how you are going to deliver your message. It is easy to produce colourful, attractive CBT packages that don't meet your real needs.

If you can't afford CBT and similar tools, you have to be prepared to use other facilities, not least those you can beg, steal or borrow. Piggybacking on other departments' work and facilities is not immoral: it's making best use of available resources. Programmers call this 'object reuse'.

# CHAPTER 5

# *Measuring Awareness*

## THE PERILS OF METRICS AND MONITORING

Measuring holds many potential pitfalls. In many circumstances, things are measured because they are available and easy to measure.

I saw a recent outsourcing contract that had as one of its key metrics 'the number of times a member of the public makes a "subject access" request under the Data Protection Act'. The UK Data Protection Act (in common with most legislation across the European Union) allows members of the public to ask organizations (public or private) to provide details of the enquirer's 'personal' information. If the organization fails to do so, or is found to be operating outside a number of principles set out in the Act, the Information Commissioner can take the offender to court. The use of a metric that looks at the number of subject access requests (as such enquiries are correctly termed) is pointless. The real issue is not the number of times someone expresses an interest in what information is held by an organization; the issue is whether or not they receive their personal information in the correct manner and in the right timescales.

In the past I have been set a target that stated 'There must be a reduction in the number of viruses detected by the company firewall.' I could have achieved this by simply failing to update the anti-virus software – although I did the right thing and told them how inappropriate the metric was.

At this point it is worth differentiating between the terms 'metric' and 'indicator'. A metric is normally a specific measure of the performance of a process. Metrics tend to be tactical and occur in the lower, operational areas of an organization. Indicators are more prevalent higher up an organization, and are often a combination of a number of separate metrics.

Some indicators that become fundamental to the measuring process may be termed 'key', as in key security indicator (KSI) or key performance indicator (KPI). It is tempting to set very specific targets based on indicators. This should be avoided, as the targets will be met by fair means or foul. The use of indicators is to indicate status. If they become targets, they will be manipulated and will lose their effectiveness.

---

**Inappropriate Metrics**

Most recent UK governments of whatever persuasion have produced target-based figures against which they wish to be measured. This has been evident in the National Health Service (NHS), when emotive subjects such as waiting lists for treatment (and the length thereof) are used to indicate apparent success (or lack thereof). It is apparent that many staff meet these targets, but often using practices that are not necessarily based on medical and clinical requirements. Some people lie to ensure they meet performance targets. There are many examples of hospitals and doctors 'massaging' the figures to meet targets. It is sensible avoiding metrics that are overtly 'political', and focusing on those that are related to true performance.

---

Monitoring any security awareness initiative should use metrics that reflect behaviours. The most effective measures are often based on a combination of processes. An example would be the number of redundant logical access control IDs residing on a system at any time. The redundant IDs are often a result of:

- line manager failure to inform HR of a staff transferral;

- HR failure to process a staff leaver properly, by not informing IT security administration staff;

- IT security administration staff failure to process a request from HR to remove an ID after a staff member has left.

The results can be caused by any of the above, or even a combination of the events. It is these broad-based measures that are often referred to as KSIs.

Other potential indicators include such multi-partite behaviour-oriented measures as:

- percentage of properly patched servers;

- time from an externally provided warning (such as a CERT alert) to actual server patching (including analysis, authorization, test and installation);

- percentage of compliance failures (failing to meet an agreed, documented process), including patches, violations, build audits and so on;

- number of accesses to information security intranet pages;

- number of queries made to the security function;

- proper use of an information security classification scheme;

- proper use of a risk-analysis procedure;

- proper application of a clear-desk policy;

- number of baseline build audit failures;

- number of accesses to illicit websites.

## GUIDE TO GOOD METRICS

There are further generic guides that can make your metrics more effective. These include:

- clarity

- decision enablement

- emotion

- interest

- relevance.

### Clarity

The presentation of metrics, particularly in graphical form, can be very powerful. However, you should never use a plain graph without some explanation. Similarly, you should generally only present a maximum of three metrics on one graphic. Any more will be very confusing. Some people try and get clever and present graphs that have different scales. Don't – Keep It Simple Stupid (KISS).

### Decision enablement

A metric should support or initiate management decisions. For example, they can identify areas that require improvement, or indicate a predicted future failure that requires immediate investment. If your metrics seem unlikely to support or initiate management decisions, they are probably flawed. It will be worthwhile analysing your metrics to see if they have this characteristic.

## Emotion

If your metrics cause an emotional reaction from your audience, you will probably be on to a winner. Emotional reactions suggest you have hit a 'hot spot'. This emotional reaction can be negative ('Why are we letting our competitors into this market!?') or positive ('Wow – we are the best in this field!'). Whether negative or positive, if something is precious to your audience's heart, providing metrics on its status can prove very effective.

## Interest

Be interesting! Whatever you report, it should capture attention. This can be aided by striking presentation (using RAG – red, amber and green – charts, or suchlike), reporting success in an open and bold manner, or reporting by exception. A turgid flow of dull, repetitive figures and graphics will switch most people off.

## Relevance

Whatever you report, it has to be relevant to your audience. Use business terms, and don't report numbers simply because they are easy to collect. Don't just say:

> The service exceeded its 99.5 per cent service level for the month.

However well this indicates the effectiveness of your business continuity and security initiatives in maintaining service levels, you can increase relevance (and effectiveness) by demonstrating how this success has been manifest, for example:

> By exceeding our 99.5 per cent service level this month, we avoided the stiff financial penalties we have suffered since the beginning of the year, and we have attracted complimentary press coverage in four leading national newspapers, leading to an anticipated increase in sales next month.

In the same way the graphics should have supporting text, so should numeric metrics.

The monitoring process is cyclical. The metrics need to be checked for reasonableness as the initiative progresses, and there should be an annual analysis to ensure the measurement initiative remains appropriate and targeted.

## MEASURING TOOLS AND TECHNIQUES

### SURVEY DESIGN

There are few better ways of gathering information about people's knowledge and attitudes than a survey. Behaviour can be measured through recording events or by the use of indicators (see above). Surveys are very easy to get wrong. There are a number of steps you can take to make them more effective. These relate closely to the five-step approach as discussed in Chapter 4.

A well-designed survey requires a staged approach as follows:

- establish the goals of the survey;

- determine your target population;

- choose the tools;

- create the questionnaire;

- test;

- gather the information;

- analyse the responses .

The link to the five-step approach is fairly clear, in that the use of goals and objectives is common to both.

### ESTABLISHING GOALS

The goals of the intended survey must reflect your overall awareness initiative aims and objectives.

Some typical goals include:

- Target an awareness campaign to make best use of a limited budget by effectively measuring:

    - Specific department staff opinions

- Overall satisfaction levels.

- Determine the potential effectiveness for a new ETA (education, training and awareness) initiative by measuring:

- Ratings of current initiatives

- Reaction to proposed graphic designs.

The more precise the goals, the more likely it is that your information gathering will be effective. As with the overall initiative aims and objectives, precision in definition tends to provide clearer, more effective results.

## DETERMINING TARGET POPULATIONS

In many circumstances, it is obvious who your target population is. For example, you may have a department that is responsible for 90 per cent of all information security incidents, whilst compromising only 5 per cent of the total organization population. You may have a building from which laptop computers are often stolen, despite being no different from any other in physical and layout terms.

If you are seeking attitude opinion from across an entire organization, this makes the entire population your target. You may be seeking specific information on facts known by a specific sub-group. This again can be fairly obvious, such as a discrete group of technical specialists.

If you fail to identify your target population correctly, you will reduce the integrity of your survey questionnaire considerably.

Given that there are inevitable constraints on research, it is likely that you will not be able (financially, logistically or politically) to address entire populations. You will probably have to use a sample, and these have to be selected with care. Generally, the larger your sample, the more effective it is probably going to be – but a sample as small as 5 per cent of the overall population is considered to be statistically viable. The statistical precision of the sample does not increase with sample size. On the basis of sample population numbers alone, an increase from 250 to 1000 does not treble precision – the increase is merely doubled. Subsequent increases in sample size have a diminishing rate of increase in precision.

## SURVEY AND SAMPLE BIAS

Samples can be affected by bias. You often see survey results being presented as totally factual, when in reality they are totally discredited by bias. For example, many TV stations perform phone-in stunts asking simple questions (often requesting a Yes or No response to a provocative question). The results are often broadcast as true reflections of public opinion. Similar results come from newspaper surveys. These results are biased due to the target population being self-selecting. The population consists of a sub-group (readers of that paper, viewers of that station) who are either:

- stupid enough to pay premium phone rates for the privilege of responding to a badly crafted question; or

- have too much time on their hands and therefore give their attention to newspaper questionnaires.

Other potential sources of bias include:

- *Medium* – The medium used to conduct the survey can introduce bias. An Internet-based questionnaire will, by its very nature, exclude people who don't use the Internet. If your survey is about Internet use, then this is not an issue – but it's useful to remember that you can exclude people merely by the media you use.

- *Time of day* – If your survey is conducted at a particular time of day you may also exclude people. For example, you may omit people at work if you conduct your survey at a certain time.

- *Geography* – If you restrict your survey to a particular region, town or building, you may only detect local opinion. You cannot always extract an overall picture from such a sample.

- *Language* – Even if your organization uses one language in its official communications, you may find you fail to connect to many people if you fail to use their first language. This is not restricted to international organizations. There are many minorities within single countries. Also remember that you may need to produce multilingual material in certain countries: for example, English and Welsh in UK government communications; French and Vlaams in all communications in Belgium.

Ensuring the correct scoping and analysis of your target population is essential for obtaining valid results. One method commonly used is called a 'quota'. For example, if you need to ensure your sample reflects the overall population, you may find that there are factors (such as medium, time, geography and language) that need to be considered when selecting your quota sample. If you have multiple office sites, you may wish to ensure that each site is included in proportion to the number of staff in each. Failure to do so may introduce unintentional bias.

You can use randomness as a means of reducing bias, but must ensure you hit at least 5 per cent of your target population. Using a quota within the 5 per cent can help reduce bias still further.

## SURVEY TECHNIQUE SELECTION

Once you have decided on your sample you must decide on your method of data collection. Each method has advantages and disadvantages.

### Face-to-face interviews

Face-to-face interviews have a number of real advantages – for example interviewers can obtain information in addition to that set out in a questionnaire. Such information can take the form of direct comments, body language, intonation and similar attitudinal elements of behaviour. Such information is sometimes referred to as 'sideband' information. One particular advantage of such direct contact is that interviewers can seek immediate clarification of a response, and respondents can do likewise, and seek clarification of a question.

Respondents will often tolerate a relatively lengthy process in face-to-face situations, especially if the interviewer comes to them, and has arranged the meeting in advance. This tolerance can lead to respondents providing detailed lengthy responses to questions. Whilst this quality occurs via other media and tools, it is especially notable during direct contact.

One particular advantage of face-to-face interviews is that you are able to demonstrate things. These can include designs, tools, software, devices and publications. Whilst this can be done remotely (web-based systems can demonstrate software for example) there is nothing as effective as direct demonstration.

Not surprisingly, face-to-face interviews take time, and can seem expensive. As the name suggests, they involve individuals, and are thus impractical for large quotas or target populations.

## Telephone interviews

Telephone interviews reduce the time required to conduct surveys (as they remove travelling time), and in most business environments have almost 100 per cent coverage. Remember this may not be the case in some industries, particularly in industrial (that is non-office) circumstances, when opportunities for the required peace and quiet are less obvious.

There is a range of tools available to assist in telephone interviewing (developed through the telemarketing industry), which can rapidly record and analyse responses. Some of these are referred to as CATI (Computer Assisted Telephone Interview) software. They can even incorporate a degree of logic, and prompt interviewers to skip irrelevant sections. They can even react to provided answers and change future questions. Such systems can also incorporate standard questionnaire functionality such as consistency checks (ensuring that certain answers were indeed provided truthfully).

Telephone surveys have some characteristics similar to face-to-face interviews, in that interviewers can obtain some sideband information, although in a phone interview this is rarely of the same quality as that obtained by direct personal contact.

If you intend interviewing people using cold calls, you will meet initial resistance; often because of the appallingly bad image telemarketing has given phone-based research. Many people regard phone surveys as 'time-stealing' – much more so than if a person visits them for a face-to-face interview.

One major problem with phone-based surveys is that you cannot demonstrate physical items, although you can combine phone and online systems to demonstrate such things as software.

## Postal surveys

The use of postal surveys is well understood and is the core of much organizational remote marketing. Note that I am including internal postal surveys within this section. An entire industry has grown up around the practice. Just as poor telemarketing protocol has damaged the profile and effectiveness of phone surveys, direct mail has a very poor public image. The delivery of blanket junk mail is intolerable to many. Although a questionnaire received in the post has the distinct advantage of being available for completion at the respondent's leisure, it can be ignored (or forgotten) in a way that a phone call cannot. Postal surveys are thought less intrusive than surveys delivered via other media. They are also relatively cheap.

Postal surveys have several intrinsic problems. They are slow, and obtaining meaningful results will take much longer (in most cases) than direct contact. Allied to this is the fact that relatively few people respond to postal questionnaires. A meaningful random sample requires at least 5 per cent of a total population to be meaningful, and postal response rates rarely exceed 15–20 per cent. Making the 5 per cent can be tough. You can increase response rates by sending pre-postal warnings, or by sending follow-up reminders, but these inevitably increase your costs.

Postal surveys can induce bias, in that you run the risk of excluding the less literate.

### Computer-based/online surveys

One of the main advantages of computer-based surveys (and these include online and web-based initiatives) is that the respondent often performs the act of data entry. This cuts out an entire (and often costly) process needed when transposing information from hard copy forms into analysis systems.

One characteristic of computer-based surveys is that many people are often more inclined to be truthful when responding to a machine than they are to a human. This characteristic is greatly increased if responses can be kept anonymous. Sensitive issues (such as health, sexual orientation or drug use) are often best handled by such means. Given the sensitive nature of matters relating to information security, this characteristic could be used to considerable advantage.

Another very positive feature of computer-based surveys is that fact that all interviewer bias is removed. Whilst the acquisition of sideband information in direct contact interviewing (face-to-face, telephone and so on) can be valuable, there is the constant threat of interviewers introducing bias into responses.

The use of automation can also help reduce error rates, in that circumstances wherein respondents should omit a section (due to an earlier response) are actually omitted. Good tested design can eliminate human error, and ensure those sections in a questionnaire that should be skipped are skipped. (Note that it is always possible to automate an erroneous process and compound errors faster and more thoroughly!)

Computer-based surveys are still (2006) novel enough for people to complete forms out of curiosity. This effect will diminish, but should be taken advantage of in the meantime.

Web-based surveys are booming. Response rates are high, and rapid results can be obtained. Once set up, ongoing costs are small.

Web-based presentation of information can include multi-media, such as streamed video, animation (using Macromedia Flash and similar tools) and sound. As a means of presenting demonstrations, web-based techniques are only really surpassed by face-to-face interviews.

Web-based surveys can provide very rapid results. A survey questionnaire posted on a website can gather many responses within a few hours. It is also possible to elicit additional responses by sending reminder e-mails. The process, once established, does not increase in costs.

For some reason, respondents provide lengthier answers to open questions on web-based surveys than other self-administered surveys.

The main downside of web-based surveys is that the population sample capable of responding is limited to Internet users. Whilst this section of society is broadening, it is not a true sample. It is difficult to control how many times a respondent completes forms (although it is possible to use secure web pages and the like, but this increases administration and set up costs considerably). You can limit multiple responses by hosting the survey on a page that can only be addressed directly, that is, there are no links to it from anywhere else. If the survey is too lengthy, respondents will quit before completing the questions. It is important to remember that web users read and assimilate information in a way that differs considerably from readers of text on paper (see 'Intranets and other web-based media' in Chapter 6 regarding writing for the web).

This downside is completely negated if your survey is looking for Internet and intranet users only!

One factor that seriously affects all self-administered survey techniques is that they are often difficult for people of low educational attainment and literacy to complete. This applies to paper-based as well as automated surveys.

## E-mail surveys

Just about every Internet user has an e-mail address. There are some e-mail users that do not have web access (although this number will probably decrease to near zero). E-mail surveys therefore have a broader reach than web-based surveys. However, they tend to be restricted to questionnaires rather than the more logically complex surveys that can be presented directly on the web. The use of HTML-based e-mail can introduce considerable intelligence into the message, but never to the same degree as direct web access.

E-mail shares the same characteristics of speed and low set-up costs as online and web-based surveys, and is still sufficiently new that response rates are fairly high. You can also use e-mail attachments to augment the survey, and include links to web pages, pictures, sounds and supporting text.

There is a downside – you need e-mail addresses, and you have to be aware of the increasing influence that privacy is having on direct marketing. You can be perceived as being guilty of spamming your audience, and this itself can lead to you taking a reputational hit. People hate being spammed, and will not respond to something they are not expecting or don't want.

Remember, not everyone has e-mail, and your sample will be, by its very nature, biased.

The relative strengths and weaknesses of each technique have been summarized in Table 5.1.

## SURVEY ANALYSIS

One of the most difficult tasks you will face once your survey is running is managing the results. Some surveys can be very large, and the number of responses can overwhelm the unprepared. There are a number of products that can support the development, running and analysis of surveys. Some of them produce paper-based questionnaires that can be read by automatic scanning devices. The resulting data can then be used directly by analysis software or by common tools such as Microsoft Excel or Access.

**Table 5.1   Survey techniques strengths and weaknesses**

| Technique | Strengths | Weaknesses | Other features |
|---|---|---|---|
| Face-to-face interviews | Can obtain sideband information<br><br>Can seek immediate clarification<br><br>Respondents will tolerate a longer interview process than when using other techniques<br><br>Can demonstrate physical items as well as screen-based information | Expensive and slow<br><br>Personal contact can reduce truthfulness of responses<br><br>No practical way to maintain anonymity<br><br>Organization logistics time consuming and expensive<br><br>Interviewer can introduce bias | Excellent for small target populations and revealing detail – especially if the conversation goes off-script |
| Telephone interviews | Relatively cheap and quick<br><br>No travel time required once questioner in place<br><br>High coverage (almost every target respondent will have access to a phone)<br><br>Mature technique with support tools available | No control over the respondent's environment (it may be crowded or noisy)<br><br>Impossible to demonstrate physical items or images<br><br>Telemarketing has given telephone interviewing a poor image, which increases potential respondent resistance<br><br>Anonymity hard to maintain without strong process controls | If your questionnaire is well scripted, and interviewers well trained, this technique can prove very cost-effective |

**Table 5.1** *continued*

| Technique | Strengths | Weaknesses | Other features |
|---|---|---|---|
| Postal surveys | Mature technique with proven methods and tools | Difficult to get targeted respondents to respond | Paper-based surveys have the advantage of being familiar to most potential respondents |
| | Cheap | Junk mail has given postal techniques a poor image | |
| | Permits respondents to respond in their own time | Respondents can ignore the mailing if there's no time pressure | |
| | Images can be clearly presented | | |
| | Anonymity can be preserved if required | Slow | |
| Computer-based/online surveys | Users enter data, reducing costs | No sideband information can be obtained | People are more truthful online than in person. This feature can dictate use if dealing with sensitive issues |
| | Respondents are often more truthful | Errors can be designed in | |
| | Anonymity can be preserved if required | Easy for respondents to 'bail out' | |
| | Errors can be designed out | Sample target populations limited to relatively literate people with web access | |
| | Still novel enough to encourage a higher response rate | | |
| | Cheap | | |
| | Quick | | |
| | Logic can be built in to the survey | | |

**Table 5.1**    *Concluded*

| Technique | Strengths | Weaknesses | Other features |
|---|---|---|---|
| E-mail surveys | E-mail addresses are fairly universal | E-mail overload is common, and potential respondents often ignore non-core messages | E-mail surveys combine the advantages of postal surveys with online surveys. Their reputation has suffered after being abused for years by rogue marketeers |
| | Some logic can be built in to the survey | E-mail spamming has hit e-mail reputation | |
| | Familiar tool | | |
| | Cheap | Sample target populations limited to relatively literate people with e-mail addresses | |
| | Quick | | |
| | High response rate | | |

## HOW TO CHOOSE YOUR SURVEY METHOD

I remember an old saying that states that there are three characteristics of any piece of work. These are:

- quick

- cheap

- good.

You can have a maximum of two of the above. Therefore, if you need a deliverable that is good and quick, it will *not* be cheap. If you want something good and cheap, it will *not* be quick. The same logic can be applied to survey method selection. You have to decide upon the characteristics you require of your survey. These requirements will be dictated by things other than wishes. If you have no web development capability, have no website, and your client base is elderly, home-based and sub-literate, a web-based survey is unlikely to help you.

If you are short of time and money, face-to-face interviews are probably not suitable. If your required sample is large, and you need rapid results, face-to-face interviews will not work well – not unless you have an army of interviewers and a huge budget.

If you are seeking sensitive information, you may well consider an online or computer-based option. Remember that anonymity is important in many areas (especially when trying to illicit opinion from staff who wish to criticize).

## QUESTIONNAIRE DESIGN

It is very easy to create bad questionnaires. Superficially they seem simple, but the truth is, as always, different. There is something of a 'chicken–egg' situation relating to questionnaire design. Questionnaire content will depend on the medium you choose – and the medium you choose depends on what you want to know – which depends on your objectives, which will be limited by the media available to you! I told you there's no magic bullet. If you have set out your aims and objectives, and incorporate this into your decision making, this will make the process easier.

## RULES OF THUMB

The first rule of thumb relates to all things in life. I have already alluded to it – Keep It Simple Stupid (KISS). If you are trying to find out why people abuse the e-mail system, asking them questions concerning their opinion on screen colours will gain you little. A simple filter is to determine what you *need* to know, what would be *useful* to know, and what would be *nice* to know. Write questions that provide the information you need, select with care those questions that give you useful information (question its usefulness before doing so), and get rid of the nice ones. They add nothing, and make the questionnaire longer.

On this note, keep your questionnaire as short as is useful. You might think that having massive lists of questions will add value, but remember that people will avoid filling in long questionnaires – they are also very likely to give up part way through (this is particularly easy during web sessions). Respondents will get bored as they go through a lengthy process, and will put in any answer just to get to the end, and the quality of your data will nosedive.

Once you have decided on the medium, design the questionnaire to fit it. If you use phone surveys, avoid questions that require pictures. Remember that questions that could ask for sensitive information benefit from anonymous responses, or via online media. If you use different media for the same questions, you may well find that responses vary according to the medium.

Make people feel that their responses are valued and will be taken seriously. You can do this by providing information describing what the survey is about and for whom it is intended. This information can be part of a cover sheet, a welcome page on a website, or in a covering e-mail. If using telephone interviews, the subject should also be covered up front. In a phone interview, try and avoid people reading this as a script, because potential respondents will react badly if they feel they are being treated in such a way.

All surveys benefit from a cover sheet or equivalent. They can increase the response rate and provide potential respondents with information they might need when deciding whether to complete the survey

The cover sheet (or equivalent) should outline any ground rules. For example, if you have excluded neutral response options (see below), let respondents know – and let them know why you're doing so. Provide clear instructions on completing and returning questionnaires. If it is likely that there will be queries raised by respondents, give them a means of asking questions (a phone number or e-mail address will do). The cover sheet should always state *why* they should complete the questionnaire.

You need to manage respondents' expectations. Your cover sheet should set out how long the questionnaire should take to complete. In paper-based questionnaires, it's often sensible to provide page numbers (such as 'page 2 of 5'). People are more likely to complete something, even if fairly lengthy, if they know the status of their progress. A web-based equivalent would be a graphic progress bar (this phenomenon also relates to web design, see 'Anatomy of a web page' in Chapter 6).

There is considerable debate regarding the use of a neutral response such as 'not applicable' and 'don't know'. Some suggest that it is an absolute requirement to prevent respondents feeling they are being bullied into a response, and to provide a realistic outlet for those who genuinely feel that the question does not apply or they don't know. Others feel that a neutral response is a waste, and that respondents should be channelled to seek the 'best fit' answer. If you are to use this approach, make sure you state this upfront (in the cover sheet). People will respond much better if they feel that the coercion is deliberate and designed to increase the overall quality of the gathered data. Remember also that there could be certain questions that respondents feel could impinge on their personal privacy. Providing a facility for a nil response (or a 'decline to answer' box) could prevent respondents bailing out of the questionnaire. Remember that stating this upfront will help keep respondents on track.

There will be circumstances when you provide a list of possible responses. Note that there will always be an exception, and you should provide such a facility (such as 'other'). If you provide a space wherein respondents can provide details of whatever they have, you can use this to redevelop the questionnaire should a particular 'other' be common, and you can use this data as part of the response.

Make sure your survey, however delivered, is clearly marked and that people know what it's for. You may wish to use a third party to deliver the survey, as respondents find making direct criticisms difficult.

If respondents are meant to be anonymous, make sure they are and remain so. If people are identified, you will make future surveys more difficult (and not just for yourself). If you mean anonymous, make it so. There is often value in revisiting respondents, and this clashes with any need for anonymity. Providing an option to include contact details is probably the most effective way of meeting both needs. Make sure respondents know that the information is optional or you may put some off.

## QUESTION CHOICE

There is a range of question types you can choose. Some are designed to elicit specific information (using responses such as yes and no). Others seek opinion, using what are termed 'rating' or 'agreement scales'. A rating-scale question would be set out as follows:

*On a scale of 1 to 5 how important is it that you tidy your desk each day?*

Such a question can be used to analyse opinion about simple control measures, such as a clear-desk policy. The responses are best seen in context, in that rather than measuring the different score between different questions in the same survey, they can be best used when measuring changes in opinion and attitude over time.

The results of such questions can be used to show strong opinion. An overall score of more than 4 or less than 2 shows a strong trend. Most answers tend to be centralized unless there is strong opinion being expressed.

It seems that a scale of 5 is appropriate. A 10-point scale provides little additional granularity, although some research suggests that it is useful if used in highly literate, educated target populations.

Some scales deliberately use an even number of response choices to force respondents into either a negative or positive opinion. An interim response (as provide by an odd-numbered scale) provides a cop-out for respondents, and this can flatten results. It is possible to determine scale length by considering the medium you plan to choose. The option of a neutral response in online surveys can reduce the number of respondents bailing out, as it reduces impatience. In face-to-face interviews, it is easier to use sideband feedback to elicit a less safe response, and make an even-numbered scale more attractive.

Some scales are text based rather than number based. An example would be:

*Irrelevant – unimportant – quite important – important – critical*

The scale must be reasonable – the steps between each must be clear. Providing extreme options will force respondents into the middle ground, for example, a scale using the following terms would skew responses into the middle:

*The worst ever – OK – The best on the planet*

If you do choose a scale, stick with it. There is no statistically credible way of matching responses between a 5-point and a 10-point scale.

Note that many respondents are less concerned with providing accurate answers than with providing what they hope are the *correct* answers. Some of this behaviour stems from a desire to please. Sometimes it comes from fearing that their responses will in some way be used negatively against them (note that making responses truly anonymous will reduce this). It is a natural human trait to want to agree (see the box 'The Noddy Effect' in Chapter 1). You can reduce the effect of this trait by seeking the same information through two sets of questionnaires. One set asks if respondents *agree* that a particular issue is good; the second asks if respondents *agree* if the issue is bad. Such a technique requires extra analysis and should only be used when seeking a higher degree of accuracy than normal. These are sometimes called 'mirrored questions'. It is best that a numeric scale uses the higher number as a positive response. Once you have established this, stick to it. Changing the emphasis will confuse the respondent.

Another very human trait is to provide answers that make the respondent look good. When asked, everybody thinks we should increase spending on schools and hospitals, but less will vote for the party that promises this via new taxation. When asked about personal choice of music, more people state 'classical' than is strictly true. This trait is strongest in face-to-face interviews – online surveys reduce it, especially if anonymity is preserved.

## QUESTION ORDER

The order in which questions are asked can affect both the results of the survey and the likelihood that it will be completed. Inappropriate order choice can increase the bail-out rate considerably.

It might seem obvious, but it's best to put the easy questions first. There should be a degree of flow to the questions, and this will set a mood and give the process some momentum. In face-to-face and phone interviews these early questions allow a rapport to develop. This rapport adds to this feeling of momentum.

Rapport is important, in that as the questionnaire progresses there may well be tricky, personal or embarrassing questions. These are best left later as some respondents might bail out at this stage, but at least you will have collected most of the responses. Having rapport makes it more likely that the respondent will continue to answer.

It is best to group questions if possible. If there are several natural groupings, use them to structure the question order. Randomized questions reduce context and will make the questionnaire harder to complete. There are circumstances that make random questions suitable, and this is when you want to prevent respondents relating responses to earlier questions. Grouping questions (especially if they have the same form of response) can also cause respondents to reproduce the same answer. A long list can see the quality of response progressively decrease as less time and thought is applied by the respondent. It can be worth breaking up long lists to avoid this.

Question order can affect respondent answers. If a list is presented via online media or on paper, respondents will often choose answers closer to the beginning of the list. If lists are presented orally (in a face-to-face or phone interview), respondents often chose the answers presented later in the list. You can compensate for this by having two sets of questionnaires that ask mirrored questions as mentioned above.

## ANSWER ORDER AND COMPLETENESS

Just as question order can have an impact on results, so can the options presented as answers. Many of these have a fairly obvious structure (yes or no, good or bad). Make the answer choices obvious and sensible. If you are asking a series of questions that require thought (and you provide a long list of potential answer options), it is sensible (if possible) to change the order these questions are presented for each respondent (in effect, randomising the order). This will reduce the effect of respondents choosing answers from the beginning or ends of lists as mentioned above.

Provide as many options as possible for answers in a questionnaire. If you do not, you can skew the results. By not doing so you can drive respondents into providing answers that are, in effect, extreme views.

## QUESTION TOPOLOGY AND TERMINOLOGY

Make sure your questions will provide the information you are looking for. A badly worded question will provide bad data. Do not, for example, ask two questions at once. The potential ambiguity of this will impact on the results. Make it clear what you mean. A question should never be a leading question, anticipating or preferring a particular response.

Do not use provocative terms or loaded words. I remember completing an aptitude test as part of my entry into a masters degree course. The test was questionnaire based, and included culturally-loaded terms (it was also very obviously written in the USA). I spotted very quickly that the piece was loaded, and deliberately skewed my answers. I exaggerate for effect, but one question went something like:

> *America is to good as the Soviet Union is to:*
> *Aubergine – Ballet – Evil – Ford Prefect*

Such a question in a survey situation will fail to give you anything meaningful. Questions should cover all aspects. If you ask:

> *Do you use:*
> *Microsoft Windows XP  –  Solaris Unix*

this will exclude people who use other versions of Windows, other version of Unix (such as Red Hat), Linux and all Apple users. The question will cause some people to bail out. Others will provide incorrect answers and carry on, losing patience and providing increasingly poorer quality responses.

Make sure you do not use specialist terms or TLAs (three letter acronyms) that your respondents may not know. If in doubt, leave them out. It is the habit of all professions to use short-cut terminology, and information security is no exception. They can also mean different things to different people. Look at the following common acronyms, all of which should be familiar to information security professionals – RSA, ATM and SDLC. They could be:

RSA    –    Republic of South Africa
             Rivest, Shamir and Adelman
             Royal Scottish Academy

ATM    –    Automated Teller Machine
             Asynchronous Transfer Mode

SDLC   –    Synchronous Data Link Control
             Systems Development Lifecycle

## STUPID QUESTIONS

Don't ask stupid questions. There are few occasions when you cannot, in a face-to-face interview, determine the gender of the respondent. In such circumstances, you should not ask them their gender, unless it is very ambiguous. You may have to ask such questions in self-administered surveys (postal, online and e-mail), but the respondent will understand this. In fact, do you really need to know the gender of respondents? Do you *need* to know it? If not, consider ignoring it altogether.

If you want people to provide handwritten answers, give them space to do so effectively. Providing two lines in a tightly bounded box on a paper questionnaire is unhelpful and irritating. I get really annoyed when I'm given a tiny space to write out my full name.

When asking personal details, try and collect name, address and other basic details only once. To repeat the process bores and annoys the respondent (increasing bail-out and data-quality problems).

Don't assume anything about people's names. Some people have two middle names – others have none. If you feel you need to ask such detail, do so, but provide room for all options. Remember that certain terms that may seem innocuous to you may be offensive to others. The western convention of referring to a person's first name as their 'Christian' name could easily be offensive to a Jew or a Muslim. Use broad terms, such as 'first name'.

Remember that you have to create your questionnaire from the perspective of the respondent. A case I use repeatedly is that of a friend from the Shetland Isles, who was asked if he would attend an interview to join the British Army. The Shetland Isles lie well north of the Scottish mainland. He was sent a form to obtain what's called a 'travel warrant' so he could get free travel by rail to the army depot. The form asked for 'the nearest railway station'. My friend responded (quite correctly in terms of pure distance) 'Bergen' (in Norway). Norwegian Railways don't take UK Armed Forces travel warrants as far as I know.

Sideband information is easy to capture face to face. The only way to do so using self-administered media is to leave a space for respondents to add comments. Such information is incredibly hard to quantify, but it can be extremely valuable.

## QUESTIONNAIRE LAYOUT

There are two main reasons for having a good layout. Firstly, it should be easy to understand and complete. Secondly, if it is used as a direct data source, it should be easy for people to extract results.

The best place for an answer box or space is on the right hand edge of a sheet of paper or a screen. Try and place them in the same place, as inconsistency can lead to confusion.

Layout for screen-based survey forms should adhere to the guidance provided in Chapter 6. The following general tips are worth bearing in mind:

- KISS – don't try and be a graphic designer. Remember that the purpose of the form is to gather data, not to show the world why you failed basic art classes at school.

- The best set up for clarity is black type on a white background.

- If you are using a small font (perhaps due to page restraints) use a simple font such as Garamond or Arial.

- Use simple backgrounds, as patterns and background animation can make reading text on screen extremely difficult.

- On screen-based forms, avoid moving images. This becomes more important if respondents are connecting remotely using slower connection links. Graphics can take an age to download. Not everyone is (yet) on broadband.

- Try and keep screen pages simple, and provide a single page at a time. Scrolling up and down should be minimized but is probably acceptable. Having to scroll right and left is unforgivable!

- Test your screen-based forms (if using web-based technology) with a range of browsers. You may find certain configurations have unexpected scrolling and colour issues.

## TEST

I have a tendency, after a while, to go 'word blind' when writing text. This is why I have an editor! This applies as much to questionnaires as anything else. So, test your questionnaire, preferably with people who match your target respondents. They will tell you quickly enough if you've been ambiguous, or if the form is hard to complete.

## SUMMARY

'There are lies, damned lies and statistics.' Thus said Benjamin Disraeli, Queen Victoria's favourite Prime Minister. It is very easy to make seemingly plain numbers say many things. Measuring the effectiveness of your information security initiatives has a purpose. It is not to present you in a good light. It is not to ensure you win and maintain your staff budget. Whilst it can be used to assist in such matters, its main purpose is to keep your awareness work on track, and to target your limited resources into those areas where it will make a real, positive difference.

If you chose the wrong kind of metrics, you will fail in this, and can find yourself valiantly meeting targets that are not in the best interests of your organization.

There are many means by which you can measure your initiative, but it is easy to get this very wrong. Surveys and questionnaires are time-tested tools, but they do need thought and preparation. Just asking a question is not enough. You have to think about what it is you are trying to prove.

It is sensible to link your survey tools to the five-step approach. The techniques discussed in this chapter centre on the establishing of goals. Without these, your survey will fail. If your survey fails, it is likely that your awareness initiative will be, at best, sub-optimal. At worst it will be a waste of time and money.

All the techniques outlined in the chapter above have their various strengths and weaknesses. There are no magic bullets that work in all circumstances. You will have to choose your technique(s) to suit your pocket, timescales, culture and target population.

If there is one lesson from this chapter it is that you must test your proposed tools and techniques. You do this to help you empathize with your target, and to reduce the chances of people bailing out from your survey. It's rare that you are given such authority to demand a mandatory response. Most of the time you are imposing on your targets and you have to make their lives as easy as you can. They're probably busy enough without you adding to their work. If you reduce the bail-out rate, the better the quality of your overall data.

# CHAPTER 6

# Delivery Media and Graphic Design

The five-step approach centres on the determining of goals and objectives prior to determining *how* you are going to deliver your initiative. Too often I have seen people engaged in running a security awareness campaign who dive in quickly and start discussing delivery media well before they have even worked out what it is they want to change. Popular favourites include mugs, pens, drink mats (coasters), fluffy stick-on bugs and mouse mats.

Another early thought may be 'I need a logo'. What I have experienced in this area is that suddenly everyone thinks they can be a graphic designer, understand colour balances and do as good a job as professional advertising copywriters.

Whilst there is always room for the gifted amateur, there is little better than a well-done professional job. I suppose the best approach is to take Dirty Harry's advice and realize 'a man's got to know his limitations'. You can produce reasonable copy, you can make reasoned judgements on artwork and logos – just don't pretend you're an expert!

One exception to this is when you decide to elicit the help of your target audience in providing input to the process. This has a positive effect, in that this can be part of building a community (see Chapter 4 'Step 3 – Planning'), and is part of seeking buy-in to the awareness process. You could, for example, run a competition (using something like your in-house magazine) that asks for artwork. You can make this even more poignant by asking that staff members' children get involved. This way, you engage your potential audience, you can present prizes and rewards (see 'Step 3 – Planning' regarding the 'norm of reciprocity') and obtain graphics that are potentially interesting without having to be scrutinized as serious artistic output. Media and design choices have to be made within the context of your overall goals and objectives. Just as with training needs assessment and other techniques, you have to ensure that whatever you choose meets your objectives.

## DESIGN PRINCIPLES

There are a number of different aspects of design that need to be considered whether creating a piece of fine art or producing a commercial graphic layout for an awareness campaign. The four main elements of design are composition, colour, type (or font) and graphics.

Composition is related to aspects of presentation such as layout, weight (of text), colour, spacing of elements within a page and balance within a graphic. Colour touches on issues that include colour choice and combinations.

There are other elements of design that occur commonly. These are often referred to as classic theory and are line, shape, texture, colour and space. Other principles of design include rhythm, balance, emphasis and unity.

For example, the principle is that unity in a design can be created by placing elements into a grid, repeating them or grouping them. The elements should then look as if they belong together. Rhythm is a concept whereby a pattern can be repeated to have either a calming effect (by smoothly repeating an element), or an exciting effect (by using abrupt changes in size and position of elements).

One of the key principles of design is the maintenance of graphic consistency. If you use devices such as rhythm to create variations within a broader piece, some degree of aesthetic integrity needs to be maintained. Graphic design should assist in communication; leaping spasmodically between fonts, colours and other design elements prevents clear communication, reducing the effectiveness of the presented pages, and makes learning and retention much harder. For example, if you use a particular font, colour and print weight to indicate a reference to another page, this has to remain consistent throughout. Many graphic designers develop systems to enable consistent communication. Such systems use the same icons, fonts, names and means of representing links.

Icons are another device that also aid communication; they provide shortcuts that are easier for a reader to recognize and use.

Remember that the organization you are working for may have a distinct and inviolate brand that you must work within. This may define all the design elements within which you have to work. Many companies have extremely rigid rules as to how you can use company logos, fonts and colours. Straying from the norm is forbidden.

## COLOUR

The design principles relating to colour are legion. Unless you have a serious artistic bent, or have ready access to someone who has, the use of design professionals will pay dividends if you are seriously contemplating using colour as a means of conveying your message. There are some basic ideas that you may wish to consider if you decide to approach the subject yourself.

There is a concept referred to as a 'colour wheel'. This is used to show how certain combinations of colour, tone, saturation and weight can change the way the message is presented. Colour wheels help you understand the way people perceive colour. Some colour combinations are complementary, and appear on opposite sides of a colour wheel. Blue/yellow and red/green combinations are seen as complementary. When they are placed together, they appear brighter, vibrant and dynamic. Analogous colours (which are next to each other on a colour wheel) tend to blend into each other. These closer combinations tend to be easier to balance, and are often calming and less challenging.

Certain colours (strong reds for example) suggest action; other colours are considered calming (pale blues), suggest dependability (dark blues) or liveliness (yellows). The use of red, amber and green for schemes for indicating urgency reflect what are deep-seated psychological characteristics. Remember that overuse of bright, highly saturated colours is actually fatiguing to read, especially when using screen-based media.

At the other end of the scale, blue is perfect for backgrounds, but due to the way the eye works, it is difficult (and fatiguing) to perceive details and fine screen or print elements that are blue. The same physiological traits in the human eye that make blue hard to read in detail make red and green a good choice for detail, particularly in the centre of a screen or page. Do note that the overuse of red/green combinations can severely impact on colour-blind people.

As with graphic design, your use of colour has to be consistent and fit within the design system. Overuse will distract readers from the main point of the design, which is clear communication. If you use colour coding, remember that people cannot easily use a system that incorporates more than about seven colours. Most people are comfortable with about five colours in a scheme.

As a final note on colour, remember that it can have unexpected connotations. Many cultures consider green to be unlucky. Red, green, orange and blue carry strong political overtones in the UK.

## CHOOSING YOUR DELIVERY MEDIA

In an ideal world your choice of delivery media should be dictated entirely by your goals, aims and objectives. There is no ideal world, and you have to compromise based on a number of factors. These include:

- what's already in place

- your budget

- internal rules and regulations

- geography

- network topology, capacity and 'reach'

- building layout and construction type of operation taking place in your target premises.

As suggested in Chapter 4 'Guerrilla techniques', you can reduce time and cost overheads by investigating what is already in place. If you have an intranet, use it. If you have regular management cascade sessions each week, gatecrash them. A full analysis of online facilities, e-mail systems, internal publications and management communication processes will reveal where you maximize your impact whilst keeping your costs down.

Your enthusiasm for this task has to be tempered by analysing the rules and regulations that almost inevitably surround internal communication. Find out who controls this, and make sure you don't damage yourself by failing to meet corporate standards. Once you know what's in place, and who runs it, you are in a better position to publish.

One action that is sometimes missed is a site survey. If you intend to use physical media (notably such items as posters), make sure that the physical location is suited to such things. If you spot areas where people congregate or are forced to wait (water coolers, lunch queues or lift lobbies), try and make use of them.

If you have regular 'desk drops' as a means of delivering messages, this could lead you to choose media such as booklets or fan fold leaflets. Internal costs are often hidden, so you can piggyback on such facilities and reduce your overall programme costs.

# INTRANETS AND OTHER WEB-BASED MEDIA

Web-based tools have excellent potential. They provide:

- a single point of editing and publication for volatile documents;

- a two-way interface, allowing publishers to gather information about readers (see Chapter 5 'Survey Technique Selection' on online survey tools);

- no central printing costs;

- no additional distribution costs;

- rapid changes;

- links to other web pages, allowing readers to gain more specific information.

However, web-based publication allows you to propagate big mistakes very quickly (there's nothing like a decent spelling mistake broadcast across your entire organization to impact on your hard-earned reputation).

It is also easy to create a poor series of web pages by not taking account of the different way in which people read screen-published text (see 'Web-based text' later in this chapter).

## ANATOMY OF A WEB PAGE

A web page normally has three areas. These are:

- operating system and browser controls

- content

- navigation.

The balance between the three main elements is important. It would be easy to think that the best approach is to make the content area as large as possible. Whilst this idea makes some sense, the balance between the elements is very important. Note that readers do not want masses of text (see below). Readers are not confined to a single page, and you have to provide the means by which they can easily find what it is they want, and that it is presented in a way that is readable and useful.

The requirement for operating system and browser controls is universal. The navigation element provides the means by which readers can work out what it is you are offering, and the means to get there. You have to spend time on the structure of your pages to make sure there is a reasonable logical linkage between them (remember that readers will not read through the site as they would a book). Readers must be able to find what they want, and *find a way back*. Every page should have the facility that allows people to return to a home page, and also have access to a site map. The map provides another view of your content that allows readers to access what they want directly.

Figure 6.1 displays the main features of a web page (in this case, it is a generic example to illustrate the placement of various elements). The large numerals show:

1.    content area

2.    first level navigation

3.    menu map

4.    search facility

5.    sidebar.

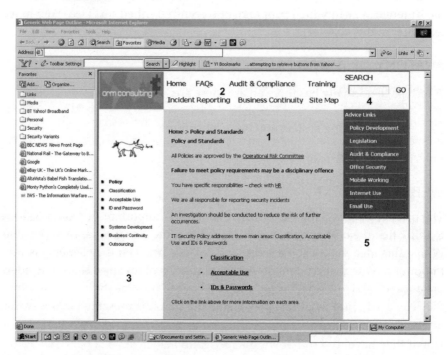

**Figure 6.1    Generic web page**

I have shown the example with the left-hand side of the screen filled with the 'Favourites'. I tend to use this option when browsing, and many sites are deliberately designed with this in mind (try www.bbc.co.uk as a good example of this).

The content area takes about 60 per cent of the usable space. It is not heavily populated, as its main concern in this instance is to direct users to the appropriate destination pages (see below for more details on destination pages). The underlined text indicates links to other content (or other sites). The convention is normally that such links are coloured blue.

The first level navigation area holds links to the main content areas of the site. They should direct you to sub-pages that lead rapidly to relevant destination pages. Common features at this level include frequently asked questions (FAQs) and the site map.

The menu map is a useful feature especially if you are taking people through a linked hierarchy of documents (such as an information security policy and its supporting documents). It allows readers to get to relevant material rapidly whilst allowing them to see and understand its context.

The search facility is a standard feature. Not having it would perturb many readers.

The sidebar is another common feature, and is normally used to take readers into related areas, often to stand-alone texts such as white papers (delivered in such electronic formats as PDF, which allow for quality printed versions to be produced by users). You can also use the sidebar to direct people to specific facilities, such as computer-based training (CBT) modules. These links normally take readers to destination pages.

## WEB-BASED TEXT

You need to condense the text length of what you are saying. As a rule of thumb summarize your original text to 50 per cent of its initial length, then do the same again. Once you have done this, try and imagine the text as bullet points. Once you have finished all this, you're getting closer to something that might work on a screen.

Web users generally dislike having to scroll up or down. This is especially true if they have to scroll down the navigation elements of a page (see below regarding navigation). Aim at using one single page for each section of content.

This is not always possible, but scrolling should be minimized. A method called 'page-chunking' works well. This involves breaking up substantial text into chunks then linking them with hypertext. It is important to remember that each page has to stand up on its own, as some readers may not reach them from a previous page in a sequence. They therefore will not have the advantage of context that readers who have followed the pages sequentially may have. The actual chunks should be indexed to allow readers to skip those pages they feel are not relevant. One trick to identifying chunks (if they are to be used with this facet in mind) is to understand the culture of your readership (see Chapter 2). For example, in an organization that operates quickly and decisively, having chunks with multiple cross references and links to other items may be wasteful. You need to identify the information people will need to find and assimilate fast. Everything else will be a distraction. A more deliberate organization that requires depth of research will benefit from multiple, linked chunks.

It is essential that you get the most important elements of the text in early – this is what people see first, and will help them make a decision whether to continue reading or not. Just as journalists provide a hook for catching attention, you need to do the same – only more so. A concept called the 'inverted pyramid' principle is used by print journalists, and provides useful guidance for web authors. A summary of the principle is to start with a conclusion (or point) in the first paragraph. If you put all the points you want to make in a bulleted list, you should assign priority based on the relative importance of each. This provides the order in which they should appear in your text. Assigning one idea per paragraph (or chunk) is another useful heuristic. A reader can bail out of an article knowing that they have probably read the most important elements.

Reading off screens is difficult, and many readers (especially men) skim the content rather than read text verbatim. If you structure your content well, and ensure key words appear (in priority order) you have a better chance of having readers stop skimming and start reading.

It is normally best to put detail into supporting pages. These are often termed 'destination pages', and are for people who have already decided they are interested in the subject in question, and actually want detail.

Avoid tortuous language and metaphors. KISS. This is particularly true of puns (they will be missed by many, especially readers for whom English is a second language). The use of humour is a matter of considerable debate – some consider it essential (and that much of the text published on the web and on corporate intranets is bland and soulless). Others think that you should play it straight. If you do use a jocular style, it should be consistent across all pages – although you may change style for destination pages.

Destination pages provide solid factual content, and may not be the place for light-heartedness. Despite this, you may have an organizational culture wherein blandness is frowned upon. Choice of style depends on what you want the content to do. If internal communications that request action are formal and if you want people to act on your content, it's probably best that you use a formal style.

There are few things that annoy web users more than 'site under construction' notices and errors. *All* sites should be constantly under construction, and telling your audience that they're missing something looks unprofessional. To avoid error, check your content. There is no excuse for spelling mistakes – I always develop text using Microsoft Word and use its spell-checking facilities. Have someone else proofread your copy. I have a tendency to go word blind after writing copy, and as I know what I meant to say, I tend to read what I want to see (see the 'Piltdown Man syndrome'). It sometimes pays to use a professional copywriter (especially if you intend to publish on the Internet – global audiences are very unforgiving).

## NAVIGATION AND SEARCHING

I've heard many web designers say that you should only be 'three clicks away' from any page on a website. I suspect this is wishful thinking, as sites that contain a lot of detail may require much more. I think that the best rule is to ensure that users always know where they are on a site, and that they can backtrack easily. Ideally, the structure should be so obvious no one need ever become lost! The keystone of all navigation is the home page.

An effective home page should instantly tell a reader what the site is about. It should also make sure readers know where they are. A good example should lead readers into obvious content pages, and provide navigation that allows effective escape from wrong turnings.

Many web designers insist on a welcome page accompanied by extensive text written by some senior executive who should know better. I can't think why people think anyone wants to be welcomed. We go to a website for a purpose. We tend not to care what the author's (or owner's) purpose is. We want information quickly and we want to know where it is.

You should pay especial attention to the wording of page and section titles and headings. If readers are using a search engine, this will pull out the various headings it thinks are relevant. Each heading and title has to be reasonably understandable away from the context of the supporting text. The titles and headings should be informative but not too long – and you should try to keep titles different, as a search that turns up with a list of similarly named titles and headings will be significantly less easy to use.

## SCREEN LEGIBILITY

### Fonts

Try to use readable fonts, such as Arial when publishing small text. Arial has no little font adornments (called serifs) that decrease screen legibility. Serifs are fine in print and for larger font sizes, but not for screen-based text. Keep font sizes sensible, and remember to keep simple fonts for the small print – not the headlines. One particular point is to avoid the use of large blocks of capitals, AS THEY ARE VERY HARD TO READ ON SCREEN. IF YOU WERE TO WRITE EVERYTHING IN CAPITALS (ESPECIALLY WHEN YOU JUSTIFY THE TEXT) THE RESULT IS AN ALMOST UNREADABLE MESS. SO DON'T DO IT.

### Use of colour

The most readable contrast mixture for screen-based text is black on white, followed by white on black. Some suggest yellow on black to be very effective, but this is not common these days. Always avoid red/green mixes, as they are hard to read anyway, and will completely confuse colour-blind readers. See the section above on the use of colour in design. The principles apply as much to screen-based display as for paper-based information.

### Patterns

Avoid too much background patterning, as patterns make it harder to read text (by messing with our pattern-recognition capability). Also avoid having moving text – even ticker tapes – as they are hard to read and often rather annoying.

It is also normally best to left justify the text as this makes it easier to read.

# OTHER CHANNELS

It is easy to be seduced by the power and flexibility of web-based solutions. Most corporations in the western world are sufficiently sophisticated to have intranets and an educated user base. There are many reasons for choosing other channels, not least a lack of network penetration within parts of an organization, or if dealing with target populations that are not predominately desk based and not habitually having screen access.

## VIDEO

The delivery of material via video is rated as being highly effective as a means of making people aware and as a means of providing training. The combination of sound and vision increases the value and effectiveness of training, as it provides two sensory routes into a participant's learning processes.

I have never seen a good information security video. Most of those I've seen are either dated or patronizing. For many years, video was regarded as expensive and inflexible (thereby prone to becoming dated). This has changed recently, and the use of fairly simple tools for manipulating video, sound and other media files is commonplace. Operating systems are now shipped with such tools on board. For example Microsoft Movie Maker forms part of the basic Microsoft XP package; it contains many features that were only previously available on expensive professional applications. Creating and distributing video as a digital file is now fairly easy and cheap. The problem is, it's very easy to do this badly, and video quality can be poor if you have a limited, low bandwidth network.

A generic information security video that meets the needs of a wide range of organizations, and retains quality, effectiveness and pertinence could easily become very lucrative.

## POSTERS

Nearly every awareness initiative I have been involved with (either directly or as an observer) has pondered the use of posters. Posters are only effective if they are actually read and understood. This sounds obvious, but many posters are either designed in such a way as to make them illegible from anything other than the closest inspection, or are placed in a location that causes them to be ignored.

I recall a security poster developed by a security institute as a means of spreading the information security word. It held about 10 bullet points of about 20 words each. There was no memorable strap line, and the text itself was turgid and pretty patronizing. It was A3 size and was virtually useless for the following reasons:

- the print colour had little contrast (mostly light cyan on white – useless);

- very few people will look at 10-point text – it is not memorable;

- it was boring.

Contrast this with the poster in Figure 6.2, which:

- has clear text;

- contains a simple, memorable message;

- is visually striking.

The poster is one of a series that introduced a range of topics over a number of months. The diamond shaped logo was used throughout the process, appearing in articles, on collateral (see below) and booklets.

However well designed, if the poster is put in the wrong place it will fail. It is designed to be read. I recall one organization designing and printing many posters, then realizing that their main user offices were open-plan, with a very strict 'no posters' rule. The posters were pulped. One simple lesson from this is that there's nothing like a site visit in person to find out what's going on. There's only so much you can do from a desk and on the phone.

## GOOD LOCATIONS

One of the best places to put a poster is in a clipframe near lift doors. People don't like to spend time waiting for lifts, and will actively seek distraction when doing so. Put posters inside lifts for the same reason. In fact, put them anywhere where people have to wait, such as where people queue for lunch, by water coolers, photocopiers and communal fax machines. I have even seen them on the inside of toilet doors and at eye level above urinals.

Do remember that if you want to avoid posters being defaced – use clipframes or some such similar covering. The frames also maintain the quality of the paper for longer – a shabby poster will reflect on your own credibility.

**Figure 6.2    Security poster**

Rotate your posters fairly often (a couple of weeks makes them seem fresh). If you are dealing with multiple, remote office sites, make friends with a local (they might perhaps be your local information security contact). Ask them to place them in sensible places. Remove posters that have a published date on them that has passed. Out-of-date event diaries on websites look amateurish. The same applies to posters (and any other media proffering dates).

## BOOKLETS

Booklets require sound writing if they are to be effective. They are relatively expensive to produce, and will only be worthwhile if people retain them. There are two simple ways this can be done: the first is to ensure the booklet is printed on quality paper; the second is to provide reference material, such as lists of contact details – phone numbers, e-mail addresses and web links. Good writing is hard to achieve, so using a specialist copywriter can make a difference, albeit an expensive difference.

I recall creating a booklet that had a quality card cover, was written by a professional, had graphic content designed by a quality designer and contained reference information. After a year, two-thirds of the booklets had been retained – double what was hoped for.

Remember that booklets have a limited lifespan (especially if they contain reference information) and will have to be updated.

A booklet provides an opportunity to expand on a subject, but this should not be an excuse for wordiness. Target your content to your goals, aims and objectives.

## FAN LEAFLETS

Fan leaflets (normally printed on A4 paper and folded into three) provide an alternative to a booklet. They are cheap to produce, but do suffer from a lack of space. Many writers fall into the trap of trying to get as much information onto a leaflet as possible. This will often backfire, as a crowded, wordy leaflet will simply not be read by many of your target audience. The contents should be pithy, and reflect your goals, aims and objectives. If there are a few specific behaviours you are targeting, it is these that should form the basis of your content headers.

Fan leaflets are essentially disposable media, but will need to be revised regularly if they are to remain effective and reissued periodically, or as part of an ongoing process, such as an induction programme.

## PAPER NEWSLETTERS

Paper newsletters are falling in popularity amongst professional internal communications specialists. This perhaps reflects the relative inflexibility of paper when compared to web-based media. Many recipients can feel overwhelmed by the quantity of unsolicited material that hits their desks, and a newsletter can add to this. A paper newsletter can be very effective in a distributed environment where intranet penetration is limited, provided some basic requirements are met:

Don't crowd the page with words. Remember that the purpose of awareness is to deliver key messages, and wordiness will stop many people from reading a piece.

Write concisely and clearly. Consider the use of professionals (remembering that you may have colleagues in your organization with strong writing skills).

Try and establish a community, and look for opportunities to obtain feedback, such as competitions or a feedback column. Many publications use regular feature columns (such as Back Bytes in Computer Weekly) to attract and retain readers. Such columns are often irreverent and funny, and this adds to their attraction. A gossip column can also help build a community in a similar manner.

## COLLATERAL

As with posters, most people starting an awareness initiative decide early on that they need some sort of business gift, such as mouse pads, pens, fluffy bugs and so on, to accompany their work. Indeed, some thinking never goes beyond the medium in question. These products have their place, and can be a useful addition to the armoury, but are not an end in themselves (see Chapter 4, the 'norm of reciprocity').

The following points provide some tips on their use:

- Make them classy enough for people to want them – blanket coverage will result in them becoming part of the background.

- Make them so that people will keep them – memo holders are useful, as are staplers, mouse mats are ten a penny, and the ubiquitous fluffy bug is worthless (unless you use them ironically).

- Brand the gifts so that they are seen in the context of the broader programme – they are support, not an end in themselves.

## EVENTS (ROADSHOWS, BRIEFINGS AND SEMINARS)

One of the first things many people plan when embarking on an awareness initiative is some sort of event. These range from complex, multi-location roadshows to a small stand in the entrance hall of a building that is manned as part of a 'security day' or some such similar undertaking.

Events have their place, and can provide a useful opportunity to distribute collateral, launch newsletters and highlight intranet addresses. They do not work well in isolation, and should not form the core of a programme – but they can be integral to an initiative roll out.

Events provide an opportunity to get things very wrong, and can make a well-planned initiative look tacky unless they are well constructed.

Events should form part of a greater whole. Relying on them exclusively is often a poor investment. They can, however, allow you to reach a distributed audience, and permit that rarest of things – head office actually visiting sites on the edge of organizations. The physical presence of people (rather than presenting over an intranet) is reassuring and makes the audience feel that they matter. This will increase the effectiveness of the messages you want to impart.

A briefing gives the opportunity to present a subject in detail (this can be important when dealing with some technical issues), but it is best that the audience is voluntary. Mandatory attendance at a briefing may seem a good idea, but there are few better ways of alienating an audience than making their presence imperative. Given the manner in which security is often perceived, coercion is probably a sub-optimal approach.

A seminar strikes me as being rather more cerebral than a roadshow, and suggests that the content and style may be slightly academic. If your potential audience is likely to respond to an in-depth event that presents some intellectual challenge, a seminar may be an effective means of communicating information (both ways).

## MEDIA EFFECTIVENESS

There has been ongoing debate for many years as to which media are the most effective for use in an awareness initiative. Academics (notably Kozma and Clark, two men who engaged in massive public debate from the early 1980s onwards) argued at length regarding how one medium compares with another. The results suggest that whilst comparison is difficult, it is the message that is important rather than the medium itself. Allied to this is the realization that it is the instructional method that is important rather than the delivery medium. For example, role-play and educational gaming (both of which can be performed during face-to-face training and in online instruction) *do* make a difference.

There are problems associated with comparing media, because if you want to compare two things empirically, all other things have to be constant. Therefore you need to make sure that any instructional methods used are the same.

What results is a simple message: it is content and the instructional method that dictates effectiveness. The medium used is largely irrelevant.

This leads to further debate: which media should I choose? As previously stated, the choice is resolved by looking at a number of factors, including:

- what's already in place
- your budget
- internal rules and regulations
- geography
- network topology, capacity and 'reach'
- building layout and construction
- the type of operation taking place in your target premises.

All these combine to guide you to decide what to use. If you have a large potential audience spread across three countries, no spare manpower and you need to do something quick – an intranet-based solution (should you have an intranet) seems a strong contender. It is not constrained by geography, requires the same development investment for 10 people as it does for 10 000 and does not require an army of people to present the message. In short, it is not the medium that selects itself; it is all the other factors that select the medium. Remember: there is no panacea, and no single answer. Table 6.1 provides some comparisons between different media types.

**Table 6.1    Media type comparison**

| Media | Strengths | Weaknesses | Other Features |
|---|---|---|---|
| Intranet | Two-way communication<br><br>Can accommodate multi-media for delivery of multiple messages<br><br>In common use and can be developed to common standards using common tools<br><br>Cheap to extend once infrastructure in place | Requires specialist support<br><br>Expensive to set up from scratch<br><br>Variable connectivity can reduce overall impact in a distributed organization | An intranet is very powerful if used well<br><br>It can become a very public display of incompetence if badly implemented |
| Video | Highly rated by various expert groups<br><br>A combination of sound and vision increases the learning effectiveness of the medium<br><br>Deliverable via many routes (VHS tape, DVD, digital files such as MPEGs and AVI files)<br><br>Delivery to TV screen a well-accepted medium | Expensive<br><br>Easy to do very badly<br><br>Digital files, if of reasonable quality, can be very large | Video is becoming cheaper, and various applications for manipulating them are becoming easier to use (Microsoft Movie Maker is freely available as part of Windows XP) |
| Posters | Well accepted and can have a high, if local, impact<br><br>Can be cheap to produce<br><br>Images can be clearly presented | If badly designed, can be totally ineffective<br><br>Static medium<br><br>Potentially subject to abuse and damage<br><br>Require regular changing to keep the message fresh | Printing limited numbers of posters is becoming cheaper, although there are real economies of scale in large print runs if using high quality techniques, such as lithographic printing |

**Table 6.1** *continued*

| Media | Strengths | Weaknesses | Other Features |
|---|---|---|---|
| Booklets | Can provide a steady reminder of your messages if retained<br><br>Can act as a reference source, increasing usage and message reinforcement<br><br>Can provide detailed, structured information that is not suitable for screen/web delivery<br><br>Will remain available should systems go down | Easily ignored and discarded if felt to not be of use<br><br>Expensive to do well<br><br>Can require multiple versions depending on language/literacy rates within target audience to be effective | If you want people to retain booklets, include reference material in it (phone numbers, intranet URLs and so on)<br><br>If the booklet uses quality materials (a card cover for example) it is more likely to be retained than one that uses recycled lightweight paper. This quality, inevitably, costs more |
| Fan leaflets | A familiar tool<br><br>Cheap<br><br>Quick<br><br>Can act as a desk-based reminder of your messages | Easy to throw away if thought useless<br><br>Small size makes them unsuitable for detailed information | Fan leaflets are short-term deliverables. They rarely last, and are often disposed of quickly. Keep them succinct and direct. Cramming information into small spaces does no one any favours. If writing a weighty tome, create a booklet rather than a leaflet |

**Table 6.1**    *conlcluded*

| Media | Strengths | Weaknesses | Other Features |
|---|---|---|---|
| Paper newsletters | Can act as a two-way medium (albeit rather slower than an intranet in terms of reaction times)<br><br>Can help build a community, regardless of network connectivity and geography | Easy to ignore and dispose of<br><br>Requires regular input and management to retain momentum<br><br>Difficult to do well | Many corporate communications professionals are disparaging of newsletters. This may be because they are less than fashionable due to newer media<br><br>A good newsletter can reach targets where there is no network connectivity. |
| Events | Provides the opportunity for physical presence – increasing the effectiveness of the initiative<br><br>A good channel for delivering reference material and collateral<br><br>Can provide an opportunity for delivering detail to interested people | Expensive<br><br>Easy to do badly<br><br>Episodic | Events should form part of a contiguous whole<br><br>They are rarely effective in isolation, and have to take place in a broader context<br><br>Many practitioners rely overly on what is an episodic event |

## SUMMARY

Your choice of delivery media depends on many factors. Some of these may well be outside your control, such as the number and types of communication channels available within your organization. Others will fall inside your control, and these will for the most part be based on the aims, goals and objectives you set for your awareness initiative.

The skills and talent required to provide effective design and branding are undoubtedly specialist. These creative skills are rare, especially so when needed in combination with technical skills. This is why good web designers are paid well. There are some sound guidelines on web design, so you can become effective without having to employ expensive creative help, but top-of-the-range design does provide something extra, however intangible.

Media choice normally focuses on what is effective in each particular environment. Physical location and building type will to some extent dictate what you can and cannot use. A simple site visit can prevent making some very basic mistakes, such as providing posters for locations that do not allow them.

It is easy to focus on media, and very easy to start spending money on business gifts and similar collateral before you have finished determining exactly what it is you want to do. Items such as business gifts have their place. Remember that they are a means – not an end. If you forget this, you will probably waste some of your budget to little effect before you have really started.

Careful analysis should help you decide on what media you think are going to be effective. The three drivers (time, cost and quality) alongside the infrastructure already in place should help you make your decision. Remember – there is no panacea.

# Conclusions

The concept of information security awareness is more complex than many people think. It's quite easy to make broad statements about how you are 'going to do awareness next quarter' without taking into account what you want to achieve, how you are going to measure your effectiveness and what actions you want people to do after you've delivered whatever it is you've decided to help them be 'more secure'.

There are no cure-alls, and the issue of reliable indicators and metrics is going to run and run until some very serious academic research is pointed at it. The diversity in cultures amongst and between organizations is such that solutions will rarely be transportable without considerable customization and enhancement for each.

The main conclusions I have drawn from experience and the process of writing this book are as follows:

- Manage by fact – know what it is you are dealing with.

- Measure things.

- Create achievable goals and objectives – and match these to metrics and indicators that relate to behaviours as well as knowledge and attitudes.

- Make as many friends as you can – and use skilled people whenever possible. You will never have all the skills needed to run a professional awareness campaign. Horses for courses!

- The secret to getting people on-side is involvement; involve people in your initiatives. Ask their opinions, even (perhaps especially) if they disagree with your own.

- Create an information security community that includes non-specialists. Information security people do not know all the answers. Remember that you often have to deal with a range of potentially competing cultures, and that your attempts to build a community must recognize this.

- Perception is everything. Present yourself and your work in a way that relates to your audience. Don't patronize, do drop unwarranted jargon and remember why your organization exists; it will not be to enhance the aims of information security!

- Be aware of the people you are talking to, and communicate appropriately. Use the right business terms in the right context, and remember to avoid excluding people. Try and empathize with your target audience. Remember you can exclude people through language, geography, vocabulary and technology. If you can't get to everyone via your intranet, make sure you use other means to get to them. If you run a competition on your intranet, make sure you provide another means by which those excluded by technology can participate.

- Take account of the internal culture and politics within your organization; failing to do so will cause you great pain if you run counter to the culture.

- Piggyback, cajole, steal, borrow and plunder. If you have a free internal resource (such as a web design group), use it! Remember to at least buy them lunch. This includes HR and marketing.

- Remember that people come to seemingly irrational decisions for reasons that *they* consider rational. Risk perception is a strange phenomenon that needs to be understood (and used) whenever possible. This applies particularly when trying to communicate risk issues to lay persons. Remember that emotional reactions to risk are in fact totally relevant, understandable and predictable. Emotions are valid!

All the above points reflect the content of this book and what is important is that you take them on board and use them in the context of your own organizations. There is no panacea, and no methodology than can be prescribed that will meet all needs. What this book has attempted to describe is a framework that can be adapted to local conditions. Whatever way you choose to take your awareness initiative forward – good luck.

# Bibliography

Adams A and Sasse M A, 'Users are not the enemy', *Communications of the ACM*, 42/12 (1999).

Adams D, *The Hitchhiker's Guide to the Galaxy*, Pan Books: London (1979).

Adams D, *The Restaurant at the End of the Universe*, Pan Books: London (1980).

Bee F and Bee R, *Training Needs Analysis and Evaluation*, CIPD: London (1994).

Bernstein P L, *Against the Gods – The remarkable story of risk*, John Wiley & Sons: New York (1996).

Bryson B, *A Short History of Nearly Everything*, Transworld Publishers Ltd: London (2003).

Chaucer G, *The Canterbury Tales*, (1386).

Computer Security Institute – Computer Crime and Security Survey (1997).

Computer Security Institute – Computer Crime and Security Survey (2003).

Dixon N F, *On the Psychology of Military Incompetence*, Jonathon Cape: London (1979).

Dixon N F, *Our Own Worst Enemy*, Jonathon Cape: London (1987).

Ellison C and Schneier B, 'What you are not being told about Public Key Infrastructure', *Computer Security Journal*, 16/1 (2003).

Ernst & Young – 2nd Annual Global Information Security Survey (1999).

Ernst & Young – Global Information Security Survey (2002).

Fischhoff B, Slovic P and Lichtenstein S, 'Weighing the risks', *Environment*, 21 (1979).

Griffin E, *A First Look at Communication Theory*, McGraw-Hill: Columbus OH (1997).

Hellreigle D, Slocum J and Woodman R, *Organizational Behavior*, Southwestern College Publishing: Mason OH (1998).

Hofstede G, *Culture's Consequences*, Sage: Newbury Park, CA (1980).

*Information Security (BS 7799)*, available from British Standards Online (www.bsonline.bsiglobal.com).

Information Security Forum – Information Security Survey Analysis (1998).

*Information Security Magazine* Annual Survey (1998).

Janis I, *Victims of Groupthink*, Houghton Mifflin: New York (1972).

Kabay M, 'Using Social Psychology to Implement Security Policies', in *Computer Security Handbook*, John Wiley & Sons: New York (2002).

Kirkpatrick D L, *Evaluating Training Programs: the four levels*, Berrett-Koehler: San Francisco, CA (1994).

Latane D and Darley J, *The Unresponsive Bystander: Why doesn't he help?*, Appleton-Century-Crofts: New York (1968).

Lewin K, *The Methods of Kurt Lewin: A study of action and effect*, (1929).

Lippa R A, *Introduction to Social Psychology*, Wadsworth: Belmont CA (1990).

McGregor D, *The Human Side of Enterprise*, (1960).

Machiavelli N B, *The Prince*, (1515).

Mant A, *Leaders We Deserve*, Australian Commission for the Future Ltd and Currency Productions Pty Ltd: Victoria, Australia (1993).

Native Intelligence, Inc website (http://nativeintelligence.com) (2000).

Nielsen J, *Designing Web Usability: The practice of simplicity*, New Riders Publishing: Indianapolis IN (2000).

OECD, *OECD Guidelines for the Security of Information Systems and Networks – Towards a culture of security.* Organisation for Economic Co-operation and Development: Paris (2002).

Paulos J A, *Innumeracy,* Penguin: London (1988).

Peters T and Waterman R, *In Search of Excellence,* Harper Row: New York (1982).

Sandman P M, *Explaining Environmental Risk: Dealing with the public,* TSCA Assistance Office, Office of Toxic Substances, US EPA, booklet (1986).

Sasse M A, Brostoff S and Weirich D, 'Transforming the "weakest link" – a human/computer interaction approach to usable and effective security', *BT Technology Journal,* 19/3, (2001).

Skynner R and Cleese J, *Life and how to survive it,* Methuen: London (1993).

Townsend R, *Up The Organization; How to stop the corporation from stifling people and strangling profits,* Knopf: New York (1970).

Voss B, 'The Ultimate Defense of Depth: Security Awareness in Your Company', article in SANS reading room material, (2001).

# Index

# Angus McIlwraith

Life is very complex, and we have enormous difficulty in making valid and rational generalizations. We either come to the wrong conclusions by making shortcuts in our thinking or we look at a small proportion of the totality, and make mistakes based on a sample that is not representative. This fact is at the root of many problems facing information security practitioners. There are many things that make them believe that the threats that matter most are externally imposed by strangers – such as hacking attacks by deviant foreigners. The truth is far different. If we really want to reduce risk, and defend the information assets entrusted to us, we have to look at ourselves – and our colleagues.

Information security practitioners are not in the business of allocating blame. The important thing they have to recognize is the simple fact that most of the truly damaging information security incidents are the result of internal action (or inaction) by people who either don't know what they are doing, or are making simple mistakes. Reducing the number and impact of these events can be dealt with in a number of ways. Making systems and processes 'idiot proof' is a great start. Training people is another. Education plays its part as well. If you have a trained, motivated, informed and alert workforce, you are much less likely to suffer an information security incident.

We need to change perceptions, not just of risk and threats, but of security as a whole. This includes the way we are perceived. This can only be done by acting and communicating effectively. This book seeks to help you do so. It is not a 'how to' manual, nor is it a weighty academic tome. It does, however, seek to impart practical experience and research that should help reduce the risk within your organization. People can be the weakest link in any set of security controls. They can also become the strongest.

The author knows that this is a broad field that is subject to constant scrutiny. He would welcome your thoughts and comments on the subject, and is contactable via email at Angus.mcilwraith@btinternet.com.